KEEPING IT HALAL

Keeping It Halal

The Everyday Lives of Muslim American Teenage Boys

John O'Brien

PRINCETON UNIVERSITY PRESS

PRINCETON AND OXFORD

Copyright © 2017 by Princeton University Press

Published by Princeton University Press,
41 William Street, Princeton, New Jersey 08540

In the United Kingdom: Princeton University Press,
6 Oxford Street, Woodstock, Oxfordshire OX20 1TR

press.princeton.edu

Jacket illustration, lettering, and design by Amanda Weiss

Library of Congress Cataloging-in-Publication Data

Names: O'Brien, John (John Hoffman), 1973- author.
Title: Keeping it Halal : the everyday lives of Muslim American teenage boys / John O'Brien.
Description: Princeton : Princeton University Press, [2017] | Includes bibliographical references
    and index.
Identifiers: LCCN 2016058249 | ISBN 9780691168821 (hardcover : alk. paper)
Subjects: LCSH: Muslim youth—United States—Social conditions. | Muslim men—United
    States—Social conditions. | Muslims—Cultural assimilation—United States. | United
    States—Race relations.
Classification: LCC E184.M88 O27 2017 | DDC 305.6/97073—dc23
LC record available at https://lccn.loc.gov/2016058249

British Library Cataloging-in-Publication Data is available

This book has been composed in Adobe Text Pro

Printed on acid-free paper. ∞

Printed in the United States of America

10 9 8 7 6 5 4 3 2 1

For Hamza, Nailah, and Shazia. Your Dad loves you.
For Ed O'Brien (1945–2015). I love you, Dad.

CONTENTS

PREFACE: FINDING EVERYDAY MUSLIM AMERICAN LIVES

This is a book about young Muslim men growing up in the United States. It is not a book—not directly, anyway—about the Islamic State, Al-Qaeda, radicalization, or terrorism.

Why do I feel the need to make this point right away? Because, according to a recent nationally representative survey, almost half of the American people still believe that there is an inherent association between Islam and violence.[1] After being consistently bombarded with news coverage and political discourse in which Muslims and terrorism are almost always linked, and with precious few counternarratives or corrective experiences to draw upon, many Americans assume that when we talk about Muslims we must also be talking about issues of terrorism and militant violence. The complex and dynamic reality of Muslim American lives is (of course) much broader, deeper, and richer than this narrow and security-obsessed view allows.

Guided by the traditions of sociological ethnography, this book takes a fine-grained and long-term look at the lives of a group of Muslim American youth growing up together in the early twenty-first century. In telling the story of these Muslim American young men, the book seeks to broaden the analytical frame, to look beyond the default issues of radicalization, terrorism, and even Islamophobia and instead ground the analysis in the set of issues and concerns most central to young Muslim American men themselves. The result is a book that reports on the *real* experience of growing up Muslim and male in the contemporary United States, an experience primarily centered on managing the competing cultural demands of religious Islam on the one hand and American teen life on the other and having almost nothing to do with the Islamic State of Iraq and Syria (ISIS), Al-Qaeda, or militant recruitment.

While there certainly are Muslims in the United States who are drawn to extremist causes such as ISIS or Al-Qaeda, these individuals represent a tiny fraction of Muslim Americans overall. For example, in 2015, just thirty-nine Muslim Americans out of an estimated population of around 3 million were linked to plots to attack American civilians in the United States. These individuals represented about 0.001 percent of all American Muslims.[2] Because this study is concerned with understanding the everyday lives of more or less typical Muslim American young men, it does not directly address those few who are attracted to such militant groups but rather seeks to understand the social lives and daily realities of the great majority of young Muslim men who have *no* interest in such ideologies or activities. In this way, the book presents a picture of young Muslims in the West who do not exhibit a strong sense of alienation, are generally happy and satisfied, and are effectively managing their complicated social and cultural lives. As will be seen, through their own ongoing efforts, and with support from their immediate communities, these young men are able to maintain a positive sense of both their Muslim identity and their American identity.

This book therefore turns attention to nonthreatening, average, satisfied, and complicated Muslim American youth as a set of people whom sociologist Wayne Brekhus would term the "unmarked"—a social group that has become invisible to the general public because its members do not fit prevalent, expected stereotypes.[3] Why should we care about these average, nonthreatening young Muslims in America? Because, as will be shown in the pages that follow, in their daily lives and social interactions these young people are constantly working to do what some insist *cannot be done*: to bring about reconciliations and workable compromises between the cultural expectations of religious Islam and those of American culture. While some people on various sides of the issue (including both Western politicians and the leaders of ISIS and Al-Qaeda) argue that the cultures of Islam and the West cannot and should not exist in tandem, the young men in this book give lie to that assertion. Not only do these young people believe that it is possible to be both religiously Muslim and culturally American, but they are living out this reality in their everyday lives already, with all of its challenges, complexities, and rewards.

Entering the City Mosque

One sunny Sunday morning in January of 2007, I walked toward the front doors of the City Mosque to begin what would end up being three and a half years of fieldwork in the mosque's Muslim community. Though I didn't know it at the time, I would end up working most intensively with a group of young Muslim men whom I here call the "Legendz," after the name of their sometimes active hip hop group. On this particular morning, I was scheduled to meet with Omar Hashmi, the religious director of this prominent mosque, which was located in a major American city that I will here call Coast City.[4] Omar was a friend of a friend who had agreed to meet with me after I explained to him over the phone that I was a sociology graduate student interested in studying the daily lives of Muslim Americans.

As I approached the mosque building, which was located in an area of town populated mostly by working-class immigrant families from Mexico and Korea, I noticed the prevalence of fast food places, corner stores, and car dealerships. At first glance, the mosque looked like any nondescript two-story office building. Its Islamic identity was only revealed upon closer inspection, thanks to gold letters spelling out the words "City Mosque" on the brick façade to the right of the glass double doors. I would later learn that the building once housed the offices of a flooring company before a small but growing population of actively practicing Muslim immigrants from Egypt, Palestine, Somalia, and Pakistan purchased and began remodeling it as a mosque and Islamic community center in the late 1970s. I walked through the doors and into an open lobby of about twelve hundred square feet, with a large prayer area of about the same size on my left. I turned to see a man with short wavy brown hair and a gray suit standing near the front desk. I said to him, "*As salaamu alaikum*" ("May peace be upon you"), and he replied, "*Wa alaikum as salaam*" ("May peace be upon you also"). I told the man I was there to see Omar Hashmi; he told me that he would call him for me.

As I stood and waited for Omar, I took the opportunity to peek into the prayer area. The large open space was covered in a light chocolate brown carpet patterned with green diagonal lines cutting across its width to mark where people should line up for congregational prayers. One wall of the prayer area, the one to my left, was lined with shelves full of small cubbyholes in which people could place their shoes before praying. At the moment, there were three men in the large room: two standing and performing prayer and one sitting against the wall to my right, his legs stretched out and crossed in front of him as he rocked slightly back and forth and read what looked like a Qur'an.

I heard a noise from above me and looked up to see a man walking down the open stairway from the second level. Dressed in a sharp blue blazer and light brown khaki pants, Omar approached me and shook my hand, saying, "Welcome to the City Mosque." We chatted briefly about my research project and my interest in coming to the mosque regularly. As soon as I told him that I was interested in volunteering with the mosque's Muslim Youth Program, Omar informed me that the group was having a meeting upstairs that very morning and that I was welcome to stop by if I wished. I thanked him and started to walk toward the stairway that led up to the youth program room.

"One more thing," he called after me.

I turned around.

"Are you Muslim?" he asked.

"Yes," I answered.

Becoming an American Muslim

In some ways, the story of my entering the City Mosque community goes back to an event that happened four years before and four hundred miles away from my first visit to that mosque. On this earlier occasion, I was standing in a sparsely furnished room, before an audience of about eighteen people seated scattershot on a carpeted floor, while being strongly embraced by three large African American men. As they each took turns putting their arms around me, they smiled and enthusiastically proclaimed, "*Alhamdulillah*!" ("Thanks be to God!") A moment earlier, in front of the gathered believers and guided by one of these men, I had made the *shahadah*—the Muslim proclamation of faith—and formally converted to Islam. After returning the warm greetings of these men, whom I had only just met, I hugged my soon-to-be wife and her father, and we walked out of the modest storefront mosque into the afternoon sunlight. As the three of us ambled down the street and toward our car, I remember looking up at the leafy green trees lining the sidewalk and feeling happy, peaceful, and a bit overwhelmed. I had just become a Muslim.

In many ways, my conversion to Islam in 2003 was not particularly out of line with my life up to that point. I had always been drawn to religion and spirituality, from the Bible stories and tales of Jesus I learned in Catholic Sunday School as a kid, to the communal ritual of "Meeting for Worship" held weekly at my Quaker high school, to the compelling notion of radical presence that laid at the heart of the Zen Buddhism I read about in college, to the ideas of divinely inspired justice that had helped to guide the movements for social justice that I learned about from my parents and teachers in elementary through graduate school. When, after college, I started learning about Islam from the woman who would later become my wife, I was attracted to the idea of having a structure and practice through which I could express the spiritual and religious longings that I had always felt. Becoming a Muslim worked for me because the religion provided me with a helpful framework through which I could make sense of the world and express gratitude for the joys of this life. I am happy to be a practicing Muslim—one identity among various other identities I bear—and feel fortunate that I was led to what I consider to be a beautiful religion through my wife.

While studying sociology in graduate school, the combination of my own deepening relationship with Islam and my interest in the complex social positions of Muslim Americans in the post-9/11 era prompted me to embark on an ethnographic research project aimed at understanding the everyday realities and practical challenges of life as a Muslim in the contemporary United States. I believed that by using the method of intensive participant observation to tap into the daily realities and local meanings of Muslim American life, I might be able to provide an account that was complex enough to both resist facile categorization and complicate preexisting assumptions of various kinds. While talking through this idea with my wife one day, she suggested that I speak with a friend of hers who knew the religious director of a prominent local mosque. It was through this initial contact that I was given the number of Omar Hashmi, and a week or so later, I found myself driving into what was to me an unknown part of the city to visit the City Mosque.

Meeting and Getting in with the Legendz

After my brief chat with Omar that day in January 2007, I climbed the spiral, carpeted stairs up to the second floor of the City Mosque and headed toward the youth room, where I had been told the Muslim Youth Program met. Opening the door slowly, I walked in to find a group of about twenty-eight kids, ranging in age from twelve to eighteen, all of whom were engaged to varying degrees in that day's project of painting the room's walls different shades of green. I looked around the room to take in the scene. From what I could guess, the kids were a mix of African American, Arab American, and South Asian youth. There was only one girl in the room wearing a headscarf, and I heard one girl ask another, "Did you dye your hair?" One short boy rolled a paint-free roller on his taller friend's back. A boy in a blue hooded sweatshirt leaned against one of the walls waiting to be painted, rolling his skateboard back and forth with his feet. When I introduced myself to the program's young and energetic coordinator, Shazia Al-Shafi, she apologized for the "craziness" caused by the painting but said I was welcome to help out.

Once the program ended, I headed downstairs to the ground floor, noticing faint tracks of green paint on the carpeted staircase. Descending, I saw two teenage boys seated behind a gray plastic folding table at one end of the main lobby. The table was situated in such a way that anyone entering the mosque could see the boys, and anyone walking into the social hall needed to pass them. This seemed like a strategic location. From the way the young men were seated behind the table and the presence of a painted sign and a stack of flyers and forms, it appeared they were doing some sort of outreach. As I walked across the lobby and came closer, I saw that this was in fact the case. "Register for MYP's Ski Trip!" a sign announced in red and blue marker. Drawings of a wool hat in one corner and a snowflake in the other completed the design. I approached the table and the boys, interested in learning more about the activities and members of the youth program. The boy on the left had dark skin, closely cropped hair, and a boyish, round face. He appeared to be African or African American and in his mid-teens, although the shape of his face and his quickness to smile gave him a sweet affect that made him seem even younger. The boy on the right had olive skin, bushier hair with looser curls, and a light moustache. Unlike his companion, he seemed a bit more wary about my approaching the table, narrowing his eyelids slightly as I came closer.

Reaching the front of the table, I said, "*As salaamu alaikum,*" to which they nodded and replied, "*Wa alaikum as salaam.*" I told them my name and that I was planning to volunteer with the youth group. Nodding and smiling, the African-looking boy introduced himself as Muhammad and his companion as Abdul.

"So, are you guys going skiing?" I asked.

While my question was intended to find out whether they were going on the ski trip, they took it to mean something different and therefore both shook their heads no.

Muhammad clarified: "We're going snowboarding."

"Ah," I nodded. "Do you guys know how to snowboard?"

They both nodded their heads yes. Muhammad added, with a smile, "But I have a hard time with the stopping and not falling down part."

I smiled and nodded, then asked, "How long have you guys been coming to the youth program?"

Muhammad replied, "For a loooong time . . . since about 2000."

"I pretty much grew up in this place," Abdul chimed in.

"I like to say that we kind of brought up the youth group, because when we came here before, there were only a few people," Muhammad explained.

"How do you think you got so many more people to come?" I asked.

"We started having more fun activities to get more people," Muhammad replied.

"Yeah," Abdul jumped in. "Like the ski trip, retreats, and bowling, stuff like that."

"Ah," I nodded. Not wanting to get in the way of their outreach work, I moved to wrap up our conversation, telling them that it was nice to meet them and that hopefully I'd see them around sometime.

"Alright, *as salaamu alaikum*," Muhammad said. Abdul silently nodded goodbye.

Though I did not know it at the time, this turned out to be an important and auspicious meeting. Over the next three and a half years, Muhammad, Abdul, and their brothers and close friends Yusef, Fuad, Tariq, Salman, and Abshir were to become the central characters in my developing ethnographic project, as well as my good friends. Beginning the following Sunday and continuing for the duration of my research, I joined them at weekly meetings of the Muslim Youth Program and also spent time with them at more general mosque and community events. The youth group meetings usually consisted of a mix of religious education on the Qur'an or the *hadith* (sayings and doings of the Prophet Muhammad), group discussions about being a Muslim teenager in the United States, and purely social activities such as bowling or other group games. While these gatherings were quite interesting in their own right, I came to realize that their formal structure was unlikely to allow the kind of uncensored and spontaneous interactions that might provide me with deeper insight into the lives of these young men. Therefore, after about four months of attending the meetings, I began to seek ways of spending time with the Legendz *away* from this setting and outside of the mosque. I hoped that this change in approach would provide me with a more holistic and varied picture of their daily lives. And indeed it did. Soon I was having lunch with them at local fast food places, then visiting their parents' homes, and finally spending time with them in their neighborhoods, going on outings to the beach with them, and even meeting the young women they were dating.

The more time I spent with the Legendz, the more a clear sociological theme came into focus. Before beginning my research, I had assumed that the everyday social lives of Muslim young men in twenty-first-century America would be defined in large part by their experiences with discrimination and harassment. It turned out, however, that the primary concern of these young men—and that of many of the adults around them—was actually the ongoing management of competing sets of "Muslim" and "American" cultural expectations. In other words, figuring out effective and sustainable ways of being both "good" Muslims and "normal" American teenagers on a daily basis was of immediate and primary importance to these young men. Motivated by how clearly this theme persisted in emerging throughout my fieldwork, I came to focus almost exclusively on the Legendz, largely because they were intensively and interactively—and therefore observably—attempting to navigate this culturally complex position with one another. The time the Legendz spent together offered a rich cache of ethnographic data in the form of interactions, conversations, and informal interviews that were directly relevant to this particular and locally salient sociological theme. Focusing on the Legendz thus became a strategic way of gathering a bountiful harvest of ethnographic data points—namely, interactions, not people[5]—with which to analytically investigate the particular social processes involved in managing what I gradually came to think of as *culturally contested lives*.

As is often the case with ethnographic work, I was also drawn to the Legendz for reasons that went beyond pure sociological interest. First, the Legendz and I shared a love of music. The Legendz had formed a hip hop group and shared a great fondness for rap music, including the albums, artists, and songs of the 1990s. My own years as a professional indie rock musician and familiarity with 1990s hip hop provided us with an important common language through which to communicate and solidify our bonds of friendship. Much later, as I neared the end of my fieldwork, Abdul and Muhammad told me that, for them, the day I first told them that I was a musician and played recordings of my songs for them had been an important turning point in our relationship. Second, I came with certain social and cultural experiences that overlapped, if only partially, with some of theirs. My years of work in diverse urban communities appealed to many group members, and the fact that I had spent a semester abroad in rural Kenya during college held particular significance for Muhammad and Fuad, both of whom had been born in East Africa. Finally, I think that in some ways the Legendz and I shared a similar orientation toward being Muslim. Much as the Legendz were working to manage the tensions between their religious commitments and the social expectations of urban American teenage life, I, a convert of four years, was working to figure out how to integrate the expectations of religious Islam with my own previously existing identities of musician, white American, and sociology student. While we certainly did not share the same social location, I believe that we did share an interest in approaching religious Islam and our other cultural commitments in a way that could allow experiences of creativity, freedom, and independence to coexist with a sense of communal belonging and rooted cultural identity.

Female Perspectives, African American Muslims, and Ethnic and Racial Identities

This book focuses almost exclusively on the experiences and perspectives of young Muslim *men* within the City Mosque community. While the experiences and stories of young women are occasionally touched upon, they are not the central focus of this ethnography. I believe that the book's focus on young men is the result of two realities of the social world I was investigating. First, within the United States there is a high degree of gender segregation among adolescent friendship groups in general, and the youth of the City Mosque community proved no different in this regard.[6] Therefore, once I had succeeded in building rapport with the Legendz and decided that their group would be the strategic site from which I would observe social processes of cultural negotiation, I also had determined that my fieldwork would focus on a nearly exclusively male friendship group. Although young women did occasionally spend time with the Legendz and I did seek out, speak with, and observe young women in the community, my experiences with them never came close to those I shared with the Legendz in terms of time spent together or depth of rapport. As a result, I felt that any attempt to use the little data I had on young women in this community to portray their experiences would not depict their social realities with sufficient accuracy or detail.

Related to this first point is the fact that even if I *had* wished to make the project more or solely about young Muslim women, it would have been particularly difficult to do so as a male ethnographer within a Muslim community. Although the City Mosque community was "liberal" enough to allow an adult male to be in the company of young women and to regard young men and women in a mixed gender group as not much of an issue, an adult male who became socially close to and familiar with a small group of young women—the way I did with the Legendz—would have met with considerable suspicion and may have been viewed as religiously inappropriate. This issue of mixed gender interaction was particularly salient because of its relationship to the social reputation of the young women in the community, much of which rested on their appropriate premarital relations with young men. So, while I was able to ask questions and write about the romantic relationships of the community's young men in some detail, to have tried to do so in equal detail with its young women would have been regarded as risky for the religious and moral reputation of these women and their families. Due to this constraint, I felt unable to gather and share sufficient information about the community's young women to do justice to their perspectives and experiences. While I am aware that their absence may give the unfortunate impression that their perspectives and experiences are less important than those of the young men, I hope that the reader can take this work for what it is—a study of how a group of young Muslim *men* managed specific cultural tension points that arose between youthful American and religiously Islamic expectations of behavior.

While most people seem to picture recent (post-1965) immigrants when they think of Muslims in America, there is a centuries-old tradition of Islam in the United States as practiced by African Americans, a tradition that stretches back to some of the earliest slaves brought to America and runs through more well-known contemporary figures such as Malcolm X, Louis Farrakhan, and Muhammad Ali.[7] Two unfortunate results of the general invisibility of African American Muslims within American media and much of academic discourse are that this deeply rooted strain of Islam within the United States often goes unrecognized, therefore increasing the sense that Islam is something "alien" to America, and that African American Muslims are often not considered part of the general category of "American Muslims." Fortunately, important scholarship has begun to shed light on these issues and elucidate the place of African American Muslims in the history and present development of American Islam.[8] Like many scholarly works on Islam in America, this book also focuses on an immigrant Muslim population. While I have subtitled the book *The Everyday Lives of Muslim American Teenage Boys*, I do not intend to construe that this book represents the experiences of all young Muslim men in the United States. In particular, this book is not intended to represent the social worlds of African American Muslims, a subject on which other excellent ethnographers are currently focusing.[9]

A final point to make about the boundaries and limitations of this study is that American Muslims are an incredibly racially and ethnically diverse population, and even in this context the City Mosque was an exceptionally and unusually diverse Muslim communal center. While other mosques in Coast City—such as "the Bangladeshi mosque," "the Pakistani mosque," and "the Egyptian mosque"—were known for their affiliation with a single dominant ethnic group, the City Mosque prided itself on the great ethnic and racial diversity of its community. The Legendz reflected both this diversity and that of Coast City itself. With their ranks including two Jordanians, two Sudanese, two South Asians, and one Somali, the Legendz seemed in some ways a microcosm of a global Muslim population. Their individual nationalities and ethnic identities occasionally cropped up in everyday interaction as subjects for light-hearted teasing but could also serve as points of pride, as when Muhammad and Fuad celebrated the fact that Barack Obama's father was African, or when Yusef and Abdul excitedly recounted their attendance at an event called "ArabFest." Generally, however, issues of ethnicity and nationality were rarely at the forefront of group members' exchanges. For the most part—and perhaps not surprisingly, given their active identification as Muslims—the young men's shared Islamic practice and identity seemed far more salient during the time they spent together than did their various ethnicities or nationalities. This does not mean that ethnicity and nationality never arose in their conversation, because they did, but rather that they were not particularly powerful social factors in their day-to-day interactions with one another, and for this reason they do not play a major role in this story.

Muslim American Youth as American Teenagers

This book explains in detail how the Legendz, with the support of their families, friends, and mosque community, worked to negotiate their culturally contested teenage years and together found sustainable yet imperfect ways to be religiously Muslim and culturally American teenagers in the modern United States. In telling their story, the book strives to make a central but unfortunately still-novel point about young Muslims in America, namely, that in their constant negotiations over lifestyle options, ongoing efforts to construct desirable identities, and fundamental concerns about social acceptance and being cool, young American Muslims are as thoroughly and fundamentally *teenagers*—and American teenagers, at that—as they are Muslims. Part of this book's aim is thus to propose that despite the historically rooted and still-dominant tendency to treat Islamic religiosity and Muslim identity as all-encompassing and centrally motivating master statuses,[10] it is more empirically accurate and analytically productive to consider young Muslims as first and foremost *young people*—with all of the concerns, predilections, and challenges that this social category suggests—while also looking at the particular ways in which these individuals engage with the cultural rubrics associated with religious and cultural Islam in their teenage years and beyond.

In the course of conducting the research and fieldwork for this book, I frequently shared what I was discovering with my (usually) non-Muslim colleagues. It was remarkable how often they responded to reading my field notes about the Legendz, hearing my stories about the boys, or on occasion even visiting the mosque with statements such as the following:

> "Oh, these boys are just like regular teenagers, trying to figure things out."
> "Wow, these are the same issues I faced when I was growing up."
> "Oh, this mosque is just like a normal community center."

What struck me about these statements, many of which were made by close friends and coworkers, was their tone of surprise. This sense of revelation seemed to me to be evidence of a preexisting assumption on the part of many non-Muslim Americans, even well-meaning non-Muslim Americans, that there is simply something fundamentally and profoundly *different* about Muslims when compared to other Americans.

The ethnographic evidence in this book contradicts this assumption and argues that there is nothing unusual about Muslim American teenagers seeming similar to other American teenagers, because Muslim American teenagers *are American teenagers already*. As with other kinds of American teenagers, young Muslim American men work to manage sometimes divergent sets of cultural expectations, seek forms of identity acceptable within their varied social settings, and participate in stylistic expressions that make them feel important and socially accepted by their peers.

As will be discussed, there are of course particularities that differentiate the "content" of Islamic cultural practices and expectations of young Muslim Americans from those of other kinds of American teenagers. Overall, however, this book finds that in their continual navigation of competing sets of cultural expectations, their ongoing efforts to integrate a more particular cultural heritage with a more general American culture, and their desire to feel both "cool" and accepted by their cultural community, the Muslim American young men I observed for almost four years lived thoroughly American teenage lives.

1

The Culturally Contested Lives of Muslim Youth and American Teenagers

Sunday Morning at the City Mosque

I steer my rusty green Toyota Camry into a parking spot in the lot behind the mosque. I turn off the engine, step out of my car, and walk toward the back of the white, two-story building. I yank open the heavy back door and step into the open space of the social hall, set at the back of the mosque. The large room is alive with a bustling mix of adults and children—Arab American, African immigrant, East Asian, South Asian, and a few African American and white Muslim families as well. The adults' chatter and the kids' playful noises echo around me as I weave my way through the crowd and toward the opposite door, through which I pass into the more spacious and sunlit front lobby. Here I see Thomas, a short, balding, dark-skinned man, stationed at his normal post at the front reception desk, which is positioned oddly but as usual, facing away from the mosque's front door. Thomas's face breaks into a wide smile as I approach, and I briefly stop to shake his hand.

"*As salaamu alaikum,*" I say.

He smiles and greets me in return: "*Wa alaikum as salaam.*"

"I'm going up to the youth program," I tell him. He nods and jokingly sweeps his arm dramatically in the direction of the staircase, as if I don't already know where to go. I swing around to my right and climb the winding, carpeted stairs to the second level, where I take a sharp right turn, walk a few steps, and push open the door to the youth room.

This room is even noisier than the social hall, with about thirty-five middle and high school–aged kids sitting and talking in various clusters. I scan the width of the space for a particular group of boys but don't see them. I consider the possibility that they're late today, which would not be surprising. Suddenly, I hear a voice from my left call out, "Hi, John!" I look over to see Miriam and Sana, two of the youth program's older members, sitting side by side and waving to me. Today both of them are wearing their curly hair tucked under intricately decorated black *hijabs,* or headscarves. I wave back and say hello. Just then, Farah, one of the youth program's leaders, crosses in front of me and says to someone else, "Are they in there?" I figure she might be referring to the "they" for whom I'm also looking, so my eyes track her as she walks toward the door to the youth program office—a small box of a room off the main youth room—and opens it. I peer around her and catch a glimpse of Muhammad and Yusef, perched on the edge of the desk at the back of the office. As Farah walks into the room, I slip in behind her. Yusef sees me and says, "What's up, John?" and the other boys follow suit. Each of them gives me "dap"—a combination of a handclasp and half-hug—and says, "*As salaamu alaikum*" as they do. It took me a while to get the mechanics of this particular greeting down. But now, about a year into my time at the mosque, it's become habitual.

Sitting on the large black desk at the back of the room, their legs dangling and swinging, are five teenage boys: Yusef, Ali, Muhammad, Abdul, and Fuad.[1] They range in age from fourteen to seventeen, are of various ethnic and racial backgrounds, and are all Muslim. I walk over and take a seat on the desk to the right of Fuad. Now we're all facing Farah, who stands directly in front of us, her eyebrows raised in an expression of stern expectation.

"Are you guys ready?" she asks. I ascertain that the boys are supposed to be preparing some sort of presentation and are expected to share their work with the rest of the group in a few minutes. They are each holding small white and green books of the hadith—abbreviated collections of the sayings and behaviors of the Prophet Muhammad authenticated by the ninth-century Islamic scholar Muhammad al-Bukhari, among others.

As if to reassure the group, Muhammad says, "We're just doing the five pillars. It's Sunday School stuff!"

I say, "You guys have to do the five pillars?"

Yusef says, "Yeah, it's a hadith about the five pillars."

From my own experience with Islam, I know that the "five pillars" are considered the core religious obligations of Muslims and include an initial proclamation of faith (the shahadah); prayer five times per day (*salat*); the paying of alms to the poor (*zakat*); ritual fasting during the month of Ramadan (*sawm*); and the pilgrimage to Mecca (*Hajj*), which includes walking seven times around the *Kaaba*, a cube-shaped holy site. The review and reinforcement of the five pillars is often a standard activity within Muslim youth programs such as this one.

The boys speak rapidly, trying to determine which of them will present which of the five pillars to the larger group.

"Okay, I'm doing shahadah," Yusef says.

"I'll do fasting," Ali volunteers, adding with a shrug, "That's easy—Ramadan."

"Okay, who's doing prayer?" asks Yusef.

Muhammad raises his hand: "I'll do it."

Yusef replies, "Okay," then turns to the remaining two boys.

Abdul says, "I'll do Hajj."

Fuad follows with, "I'll do zakat. That's easy; just giving money to the homeless. What is it—like 25 percent?"

"No," I tell him. "It's lower, like 2.5 percent."

"Oh," he replies.

Farah looks at me with a smile and says, "Okay, you're in charge," and leaves the office.

Adopting a tone that suggests it's time to get down to business, Yusef turns to the others: "Okay, you guys. We gotta get this straight." He raises the small book in front of his face and reads with sincerity: "These are the five pillars as recorded by . . . Bu-kar-i." He stumbles over the name a little.

Fuad asks, "Bacardi?" Abdul and Muhammad crack up.

Yusef says, "Come on, you guys!" Then he pronounces it more carefully, using his native Arabic: "Bukhari . . . Bukhari . . . Okay. . . . After I read this introduction, we can each read the part about our pillar and then say whatever we want to add about it."

They do a quick rehearsal. Ali reads the part of the hadith about shahadah and then adds, "This is the declaration of faith. The beginning of everything."

Next, Muhammad reads the section about prayer and says, "You should do this five times a day."

Yusef looks at Muhammad, frowns thoughtfully, and offers, "You could say that if people think it's hard to pray five times a day that they should be thankful because it was going to be fifty times, but Prophet Muhammad went to the Prophet Mousa [Moses] and said, 'My people cannot pray fifty times.' So, it could have been fifty."

Muhammad responds, with friendly aggravation, "Man, you got that from Omar!" He is referring to Omar Hashmi, the mosque's religious director, who often gives lessons on Islamic education as part of the youth program. Many community members refer to Omar as the *imam*, or religious leader, of the mosque.

"So?" says Yusef, slightly defensively. "It's a good story so people understand that it's not that hard to pray five times a day."

"Man, you're like a baby Omar!" says Muhammad, smiling.

Fuad reads the passage about fasting and adds, "This is what we do during Ramadan."

Abdul reads the section describing Hajj and states, "Hajj is a pilgrimage." There's silence as if the others are expecting more, but when Abdul remains quiet, the others start to laugh.

"That's it?" asks Fuad.

"Um, you walk round the box seven times," Abdul adds. When everyone laughs loudly and hoots disapprovingly, he continues, "Okay, okay, it's a pilgrimage to the House of God, and you walk around the black box seven times . . . and I'm not talking about the cable box."

Everybody cracks up. "Come on, Abdul!" cries Yusef, with an undertone of genuine frustration with his brother.

"Okay, okay," Abdul replies. "You walk round the Kaaba seven times." This seems to appease Yusef and everyone else.

Finally, Fuad reads the section about zakat, concluding, "This is when you give money to the homeless . . . or to me?" He smiles.

Farah opens the door and calls in, "Okay, you guys, it's almost time to go."

As the door closes again, Yusef looks around at the others: "Okay, are we straight?" He channels his nervous energy into a quick spinning dance move in the center of the office and remarks: "Hoo! That was like the Jackson Five."

As we all gather and walk toward the door to the larger youth program room, I elbow Abdul and say in a teasingly accusatory tone, "Around the box seven times?"

Abdul smiles and nods: "I'm gonna say that."

Ali eggs him on, "Yeah, yeah, you should really say that!"

"No, come on, you guys!" Yusef interjects with a flash of serious aggravation.

"See, he's like a little Omar," Muhammad says to the other three.

In response, Yusef unbuttons his khaki Dockers and tucks his blue and white–striped button-down shirt deep into his pants so that he can pull them comically high. "Here we go," he says, in a mock-nerdy voice.

"Oh, no!" Muhammad and the other boys cry out, laughing hard.

As Yusef readjusts his clothing back to normal in preparation to step out the door and the group's laughter dies down, Muhammad turns and faces his friend directly with a quizzical, thoughtful look on his face. "I don't understand, Yusef," he says. "How are you an athlete, a math nerd, a rapper, a gangster, and an imam?" Yusef looks straight back at him with a bemused smile and shrugs his shoulders. They turn and walk through the open door together.

––––

Muslim Young Men and Muslim American Lives

This book tells the story of a group of young men growing up together in early twenty-first-century America. At the time of my fieldwork, the friends at the center of the story—whom I call the "Legendz" after the name of their sometimes active hip hop group—were urban American teenagers and second-generation immigrants. They attended large and diverse public schools, were exposed daily to mainstream American media and pop culture, and lived in a multi-ethnic, working-class neighborhood in a major city in the United States. This social location meant that these young men faced expectations from school peers, community friends, and each other to engage in cultural practices, styles, and discourses associated with modern urban American teenage life, including hip hop music and fashion, dating and romantic love, personal independence and autonomy, and a low-key presentation of ethnic identity. In other words, they were expected to live a social and cultural life that was recognizably adolescent American. These young men were also at the very same time self-identified and practicing Muslims embedded in a tight-knit religious community. This social location meant that they were expected by parents and community adults, peers, and sometimes each other to meet the religious and social obligations of Muslims as understood within their local context, including praying five times daily, attending the mosque, fasting for Ramadan, abstaining from premarital dating and sexual intercourse, avoiding consumption of alcohol and drugs, limiting their exposure to potentially profane pop culture, and identifying as Muslims in public. In other words, they were expected to live a religious and cultural life that was recognizably Muslim. As some of the central cultural expectations associated with urban American teenage life were understood to be in tension with or even direct opposition to those locally associated with being a "good Muslim," these young men led what I call *culturally contested lives*. As such, the everyday lives of the Legendz were characterized in part by the presence of two competing sets of cultural expectations, or what I will call *cultural rubrics*: urban American teen culture, as manifested in their schools, peer groups, and the media they consumed, and religious Islam, as locally practiced in their mosque and by their families.

Because of this complex social position, the Legendz often faced practical situations of cultural tension in their everyday lives. The cause of this tension did not lie in any inherent or fundamental incompatibility between Islamic and American youth cultures but rather in the way that particular elements associated with each culture were often *treated* as fundamentally incompatible with or in opposition to one another by individuals who were socially significant to the Legendz—parents, religious leaders, other Muslim youth, friends at school, and, sometimes, themselves. When individuals who were important to the Legendz repeatedly emphasized alleged incompatibilities between specific aspects of religious Islam and specific aspects of American youth culture, a tangible sense of cultural tension could be perceived in these young men's lives.

When the Legendz came up against these situations of cultural tension as they moved through their daily lives—situations that were usually centered around popular music, romance and dating, ritual commitment, and the presentation of Muslim identity in public—it could seem to them that the appropriately "Islamic" behavior or course of action was directly in conflict with the culturally "American" behavior or response. At these points, the Legendz faced a practical cultural dilemma: If they took the more culturally "American" adolescent course of action, they risked falling short of local expectations of acceptable Islamic religiosity and identity. If they took the more Islamically appropriate route, they risked losing their status as "cool" and culturally American urban teenagers. In response to these recurring and vexing dilemmas, the Legendz worked together to come up with and utilize an array of practical strategies for the management of their culturally contested lives. They used and adapted tangible cultural materials, adopted and altered recognizable modes of speech, embraced and amended locally meaningful embodied practices, and both invoked and rejected particular aesthetic genres in subtle and ongoing efforts to signify complex identities, perform multiple and shifting states of belonging, and reveal themselves as both sufficiently "Islamic" and acceptably "American." Precisely how these young Muslim American men innovated and applied these creative social solutions to their immediate cultural dilemmas, and how these efforts marked them as fundamentally similar to a broad range of other American teenagers, is the focus of this book.

EVERYDAY ISLAM AND YOUTH CULTURE IN THE LIVES OF THE LEGENDZ

At the heart of the Legendz's friendship group were two pairs of brothers, Muhammad and Fuad, and Yusef and Abdul. The two older brothers—Muhammad and Yusef—first became friends at the age of nine while attending Qur'an classes at the City Mosque's "Sunday School." Over time, they and their wider families grew so closely intertwined and familiar that by the time I met them eight years later, all four of the boys referred to each other as "brothers," regularly spent time in each other's homes, and were alternately cared for and gently scolded by each other's parents. Both families had immigrated to the United States when the boys were quite young, Muhammad and Fuad's family (the Abdulkarims) from Sudan, and Yusef and Abdul's (the Hussainis) from Jordan. In the United States, the boys' families were all solidly working class, with their parents employed as taxi drivers, daycare providers, and social workers, and the boys attended large and diverse urban public schools. A central activity in their lives was regular participation in the Muslim Youth Program (MYP) housed at the City Mosque. It was in this context that they also pulled a few other young Muslim men closely into the orbit of their friendship circle, most notably two South Asian youths named Tariq and Salman, as well as a Somali young man named Abshir.

The particular form of Islam taught to the Legendz was shaped by and filtered through various historical and social forces, most notably the worldwide Islamic revival of the 1970s and 1980s, which emphasized a return to basic texts (i.e., the Qur'an and the hadith) and practices (e.g., prayer and fasting)[2]; the City Mosque leadership's flexible approach to the interpretation of issues such as gender and music; and their parents' desire to raise their children as "good Muslims" who would maintain the minimum local requirements of that identity. For the Legendz, the cultural rubric of religious Islam took institutional and social form in their lives through their participation in the mosque, their family homes, and, to some extent, their friendship group. Among its other functions, the City Mosque served as a space where the culture of religious Islam was visibly present and alive, manifested in the call to prayer heard five times a day, when people would stop other activities and move toward the prayer area; in the prayer area itself, which was set off from the main lobby and held an ornate chandelier and framed selections of the Qur'an written in calligraphy; in the hijab worn regularly by some women and during prayers by all of them; in the Qur'anic verses (*suras*) recited together by the youth group at the end of their gatherings; in the names of young people called out across the lobby or playground outside ("Yusef!", "Omar!", "Aziz!", "Yasmin!", "Sara!", "Noor!"); in the warm greetings of "*As salaamu alaikum*" as people met one another in the social hall; and in the lectures of mosque elders Dr. Mubarak and Dr. Nasr as they spoke about an Islamic approach to bioethics or introduced new converts to the life of the Prophet Muhammad, their words ringing out through the lobby, amplified by a slightly too loud microphone.

The cultural rubric of religious Islam, as it was locally manifested, was also present in the homes of the Legendz's families. It was evident in the "*Bismillah*" ("In the name of God") spoken before eating; in hangings on the wall that depicted mosques in Medina or the ninety-nine names of *Allah* (God) in Arabic calligraphy; in the prayer rugs rolled up by those walls; in the call to prayer that resounded from a clock in the shape of a mosque; in a mother's question: "Have you prayed yet?"; and in the Qur'an and other Islamic books on the shelf. Part of what made the cultural rubric of religious Islam so central and meaningful in the lives of the Legendz was the fact that this set of practices, symbols, and expectations for behavior was so tightly intertwined with their relationships with specific socially significant others—their families, their friends, and members of the City Mosque community.

American youth culture—and in particular the urban American youth culture of the early twenty-first century—was the second cultural rubric at the center of the Legendz's social lives. While the social power of religious Islam rested partly in its association with family, Muslim friends, and the mosque community, the social power of urban youth culture stemmed primarily from its association with the Legendz's adolescent peers, both Muslim and non-Muslim. As working-class youth of color attending diverse public schools in the urban United States in the early 2000s, the Legendz were expected to participate in or at least exhibit knowledge of hip hop music, videos, artists, and styles; romantic love and dating; parties with alcohol and drugs; MP3 players and smartphones; cars and motorcycles; skateboarding; Facebook and Twitter; urban gangs; fast food; and basketball. In addition, American teen culture assumes that every adolescent should be consistently gaining independence from his or her parents and should be relatively autonomous when it comes to decision-making and individual action.[3] These are the numerous and cumulatively intensive demands of legitimate participation in American youth culture. The Legendz were regularly exposed to these cultural expectations through interactions with peers at school, neighborhood friends, mass media, and one another.

American Teenagers and Culturally Contested Lives

People like the young Muslim men of the City Mosque who are located at the intersection of multiple and sometimes contradictory sets of cultural expectations can be thought of as living *culturally contested lives*. In this book, I will refer to the competing *sets* of schemas, habits, symbols, and practices that such people face (e.g., "urban American youth culture" and "religious Islam") as *cultural rubrics*.[4] As I define these concepts, individuals living culturally contested lives inhabit a social context in which two or more of the cultural rubrics central to their lives are highly demanding in terms of what constitutes legitimate participation, are associated with and enforced by groups of socially significant others, and are often treated—by both outsiders and insiders—as inherently contradictory. As a result, the daily experiences of people leading culturally contested lives are characterized by a high level of involvement in the active, ongoing, and strategic management of the multiple cultural rubrics that vie for their attention and allegiance in the course of their everyday lives.

People whom we might think of as living culturally contested lives in late twentieth- and early twenty-first-century America include working mothers, first- and second-generation immigrants, upwardly mobile working-class people, gay suburbanites, and highly religious scientists.[5] But another social group whose members consistently face and wrestle with multiple sometimes contradictory yet highly demanding sets of cultural expectations—though we may not always think of them as such—are American teenagers. A brief look at how the lives of various groups of young people growing up in the United States—including white suburban public high school students, African American and Latino public high school students, second-generation immigrant youth, and youth from highly religious communities and families—also exhibit qualities of cultural contestation will assist us in placing the case of Muslim American youth within the broader sociological context of modern American adolescence.

DIVERSE AMERICAN TEENAGERS
AND CULTURALLY CONTESTED LIVES

Foundational and contemporary sociological studies of high school–aged young people in the United States have usually focused on large, mostly white suburban or mid-sized city high schools and have situated teenagers in a social world populated by a range of competing peer cultures, each with its own associated set of styles and practices. The everyday labels of these peer cultures will be familiar to most readers and may conjure pleasant or not-so-pleasant high school memories: "jocks," "burnouts," "nerds," "goths," "preps," "skaters," "gangstas," "smokers," and "cholos," among others.[6] While these social categories may seem frivolous to those with some distance from high school, such labels and their boundaries are immediate and meaningful for those experiencing adolescence and often serve as the symbolic categories through which status hierarchies in high school are mentally organized and socially maintained.[7] The use of such group labels in everyday life, especially in the historically durable dichotomy recognized in most high school settings between the "jock"/"prep"/"popular" crowd and the "burnout"/"smoker"/"loser" crowd, can create the impression that these widely recognized social categories are in fact the most dominant and populous social groups within adolescent society, and that most high school students are members of one or the other. However, a close look at Penelope Eckert's influential ethnography of a suburban American high school reveals that while the "jock"/"prep" crowd and the "burnout"/"smoker" crowd are certainly highly visible and symbolically significant social groups, the majority of young people in high school fit neatly into *neither* of these categories. Writing about the school on which her study was based, Eckert noted:

> Not everyone in Belten High School describes themselves as a Jock or a Burnout. In fact, *only about 30 percent or 40 percent of them do*. But that does not make these categories any less powerful in the social structure of the school. The fundamental status of these categories is underscored by the fact that almost all those who are not professed Jocks or Burnouts describe themselves and are described as "in-betweens." . . . Most of the In-betweens do not choose alternative behavior, but simply mix Jock and Burnout choices.[8]

Eckert makes an important distinction in this passage, one that will prove significant in understanding the social world of the Muslim American youth in this book. Although prominent youth social categories such as "jock" and "burnout" or "good Muslim" and "American teenager" are powerful lenses through which young people and adults organize their understanding of youth worlds, this does not mean that the majority of young people consistently or completely inhabit social groups congruent with these categories *in practice*. On the contrary, and in keeping with Eckert's statement quoted here, sociologists of high school culture have repeatedly found that most young people *do not* consider themselves as fitting neatly into a defined social category but rather view themselves as inhabiting an "in-between" social space.[9] Instead of embracing a coherent and singular social identity, most high school–aged teenagers maintain a more complicated identity and status located somewhere between two or more widely recognized social poles. Indeed, a survey of studies of other subsets of American teenagers reveals that a vast majority of them seem to inhabit a social situation quite similar to the one described by Eckert and others as typical of the average American high school student: one in which the adolescent is confronted by and exposed to multiple socially powerful cultural rubrics but in practice works to exist somewhere between them.

For African American and Latino teenagers growing up in American cities, the two "contrasting conceptual categories" central to their social worlds are that of the "decent" or "good" young person and that of the "street" or "ghetto" youth.[10] In his influential formulation, Eli Anderson carefully specifies that the terms "street" and "decent" do not describe real groups of people, but rather "categories" that people may affix to themselves or one another and "orientations" that they may attempt to strategically adopt or reject.[11] African American and Latino youth's social location between these two rubrics—one associated with aspiration, responsibility, and morality; the other with deviance, laziness, and "cool"[12]—presents them with an ongoing practical cultural dilemma. While the cultural rubric and identity of a "decent" young person is attractive because of its alignment with academic and professional success, too close an association with this model of identity makes a person vulnerable to accusations by peers that he or she is "acting white" or is a "nerd" and may lock him or her out of local definitions of "cool." And although embracing the cultural rubric of the "street" risks consequential categorization as a dangerous deviant, engaging in this set of styles and behaviors may also be "thrilling" and carry tangible social rewards of peer approval and aesthetic pleasure.[13] The result is an African American and Latino adolescent version of a culturally contested life in which young people are faced with two distinct models of identity and cultural behavior that vie for their affiliation through their competing sets of social advantages and limitations. Ethnographers of urban American communities have repeatedly demonstrated that in responding to this culturally complex situation, African American and Latino youth often attempt to somehow move *between* these available models of teenage life, not fitting neatly into either category but rather striving to find a manageable mode of social life that vacillates between them.[14]

For second-generation immigrant teenagers, the two dominant cultural rubrics generally include one associated with "home country" culture or "tradition" and another associated with "American" culture that is often treated by socially significant others as in conflict with the first.[15] As a result, the lives of immigrant youth often involve an ongoing series of low-level cultural dilemmas caused by their location between these rubrics.[16] Such practical everyday dilemmas, which often involve choosing between more "American" or "traditional" courses of action or behavior, are frequently experienced as highly significant and consequential to immigrant youth themselves, in large part because these actions carry the potential for the young person to be interpreted by one or another party as "too American" or, alternatively, "too Vietnamese," "too Indian," or "too Mexican." Ethnographic accounts of immigrant youth are rife with stories of social sanction faced by young people who have been seen by adults or other youth as not living up to an expected authentic immigrant identity.[17] However, if these youth retreat too far from American youth culture and remain visibly and consistently ensconced in "home culture," they are likely to be reprimanded for being "fresh off the boat" by peers working to establish themselves as authentically American.[18] Adding to the complexity of the situation is the fact that the definition by parents, community members, school peers, or the larger society of what is sufficiently "Mexican," "Indian," "Vietnamese," or "American" is often vague and shifting, rooted in the mutable social perceptions and cognitive interpretations of others.[19] Thus, it frequently happens that one-and-a-half- and second-generation immigrants, like Eckert's "in-betweens" and Anderson's neither fully "decent" nor completely "street" youth, actually desire a social existence somewhere between the poles of home culture "tradition" and American "independence"—one that allows them to participate meaningfully in both cultural rubrics and their accompanying social memberships—but face the practical social dilemma of how to craft such a life for themselves.[20]

As with the subsets of American teenagers discussed earlier, young people from highly religious communities and families also generally find themselves in situations of cultural contestation among competing cultural rubrics, in which one set of expectations represents the norms, behaviors, and beliefs connected with being a "good" adherent to the faith, and the other comprises those symbols and practices associated with mainstream American youth culture and "coolness."[21] The specific challenge for young people from highly religious communities and families is that the rubric associated with being "cool" in the popular sense often calls for behaviors, symbols, and practices—such as early romantic involvement, familiarity with salacious pop culture, exposure to alcohol and drugs, and emphasis on personal freedom over institutional authority—that may conflict with the behaviors condoned by their religious tradition. This cultural tension produces and shapes a practical dilemma for highly religious teenagers who also desire some measure of mainstream youth culture acceptance and participation. If young people move too far in the direction of religious propriety, deeply embracing the full set of behaviors, symbols, and practices associated with communal religiosity, they risk being seen by less religious peers as uncool, boring, or sanctimonious, or as mindless followers.[22] However, if they move too far beyond the realm of communal religious norms, they risk losing their status as legitimate members of their communities and, possibly, of their families.[23] While there are those who respond to this dilemma by moving more deeply into either pious behavior or adolescent cool and deviance,[24] there are many religious young people who desire continued participation in *both* the religious cultural rubric and the teen cultural rubric and work to find ways of belonging to and identifying with both ways of life.[25]

CRAFTING EVERYDAY SOLUTIONS
TO CULTURALLY CONTESTED LIVES

If the lives of most American teenagers are characterized by a social existence positioned between multiple cultural rubrics and associated identities, with each competing for allegiance and affiliation, how do teenagers manage these complex situations on a daily basis? According to scholars who study American teenage life in a variety of settings, the most common way in which young people inhabit this cultural middle ground is through the ongoing, active, and strategic use of what Penelope Eckert terms "category symbols," that is, the styles, behaviors, and objects that carry a strong association with some locally salient social category, identity, or rubric. As Eckert observes, "category symbols attain their value from association with clear differences in both form and content, developing around salient social differences between the categories, and maximizing distinctiveness in visible form."[26] The category symbols that American teenagers strategically apply, withdraw, adapt, and combine in the course of everyday life fall into four loose types: material objects (e.g., clothes, cars, book bags, sneakers), behavioral practices (e.g., sports, dancing, the use of certain drugs or alcohol), cultural discourses (e.g., American individualism, religious piety, racial authenticity), and aesthetic genres (e.g., hip hop music, horror movies, punk rock).[27]

While there are some teenagers who use category symbols in a focused manner to appeal for full membership in one particular social crowd (e.g., "jocks," "punks," or "goths") or obtain affiliation with a highly visible group identity,[28] most young people engage in a more subtle and therefore more easily overlooked process of creatively applying, withholding, and combining category symbols to express sometimes strong, sometimes weak, sometimes single, sometimes multiple, sometimes shifting, and sometimes static affiliations with locally salient social identities and their associated cultural rubrics.[29] By strategically mobilizing particular styles, practices, and behaviors associated with one or the other locally salient social category, these many young in-betweens work to reap the social and personal benefits of affiliation with the cultural rubrics central to their social worlds while striving to avoid an overly intensive, exclusive, or limiting involvement with any particular one. In this way, diverse American teenagers immersed in culturally contested lives engage with cultural elements—material objects, behavioral practices, cultural discourses, and aesthetic genres—in creative, ongoing, and patterned ways aimed at managing the immediate cultural contradictions present in their lives and maintaining a tenable mode of social life and identity within a context of continual and potentially socially consequential cultural cross-pressures.

A review of previous studies of subsets of American teenagers reveals an intensive and creative engagement with category symbols that is prevalent among diverse social groups of young people who live culturally contested lives. African American and Latino youth who are caught between the possible social categorizations of "good" and "ghetto" but fit neatly into neither work in the material, behavioral, aesthetic, and discursive realms to manifest a limited participation in styles, behaviors, and practices associated with the "street" while seeking to avoid the complete adoption of a dangerous lifestyle or full membership in a deviant social group. Some African American and Latino youth turn to material elements of fashion or style (e.g., jackets, gold chains, cell phones, baseball caps) to signify "street" affiliation, even though they do not actually participate in the illegal activities sometimes associated with this social category.[30] In terms of behaviors and discourse, generally "decent" African American and Latino youth often adopt ways of walking, talking, and looking at others that signify a deeper "street" affiliation; for example, they might engage in discourse on ghetto adventurism, telling tales of urban danger in order to burnish their "street" credentials.[31] Young hip hop fans listen to this genre of music in part to experience and project a sense of "strength" and "power" and, sometimes, to symbolically "capitaliz[e] on the dangerous nature of blackness."[32] Limited involvement in the cultural rubric of the "street" holds powerful attraction for African American and Latino youth, not only because of this rubric's links with racial and ethnic authenticity and association with social popularity, but also because it allows these young people to live out what most American teenagers seem to yearn for: a lived—if temporary—sense of rebellion against mainstream society that does not entail a significant amount of real social risk.[33]

Working to navigate the cultural rubrics associated with their "home" and "host" countries, second-generation immigrant youth use material, aesthetic, behavioral, and discursive cultural forms in strategic ways that attempt to position themselves as both "American" and affiliated with their country of origin. In accounts of American immigrant teenagers of Mexican and Indian origin, music, fashion, and sports are consistently identified as cultural media through which young people seek and often achieve satisfying experiences of bicultural social life. In actively consuming forms of popular culture that include or have been adapted to accommodate elements associated with both "home" and "host" country cultures—Indian and West Indian music with hip hop beats, for example, or traditional public religious rituals from Mexico adapted to a New York setting—second-generation immigrants are allowed to at least momentarily transcend the boundaries between the different cultural rubrics that frame their lives and to experience a bicultural moment.[34] Second-generation immigrant teenagers are also likely to apply discourses associated with either "home" or "host" country culture in strategic ways to forge practical solutions to everyday situations of cultural contestation. For example, Mexican young women support each other in their "traditional" decision to remain virgins by discussing this "choice" in a way that emphasizes an American-style voluntarism.[35] Similarly, Vietnamese American women seeking to curb domestic violence in their community frame the problem as one of traditional family responsibility, thereby avoiding affiliating themselves too closely with the "American" notion of individual rights.[36] In both cases, discourses associated with "traditional" home country culture (e.g., family collectivity, sexual modesty) and those affiliated with American culture (e.g., individual rights, voluntarism) are creatively adapted in an attempt to maintain allegiance with both "home" and "host" country cultural rubrics.

Youth from highly religious communities navigate participation in religious and teenage cultural rubrics in ways that closely resemble the strategies practiced by immigrant, African American, and Latino youth. Like members of these groups, highly religious young people intentionally and creatively mobilize material, behavioral, and aesthetic category symbols (e.g., popular youth musical genres, forms of slang, and fashion) in attempts to complicate what they fear may be identities that are too "boring" or "good."[37] Otherwise devout Christian and Jewish young people demonstrate their familiarity with popular culture (e.g., movies, television shows, music, sports, and video games) and current fashions and styles to show others as well as themselves that they do not exist strictly within an orthodox religious subjectivity but are also "cool" teenagers.[38] In a way that parallels the discursive strategies used by second-generation immigrant youth, highly religious young people working to navigate dual cultural rubrics regularly frame their religiously associated practices—attending worship services, dating in a responsible way, exercising sexual abstinence, and not drinking—as the results of a more culturally American "personal choice," or even as a kind of countercultural independence, rather than as consequences of communal or religious pressure.[39] In these ways, religious activities that seem to pull against the expected behaviors of "cool" teenagers are placed within a discourse associated with the mainstream American and youthful values of independence, individualism, and personal pleasure. A consistent feature of the category symbol mixing done by highly religious teens is the negative and contrastive attention paid to those who are deemed *less* successful at such mixing and are therefore portrayed as "too religious." This constant reference to and disparagement of those religious youth deemed too "good," "boring," and "culturally monochromatic" is a means through which highly religious youth who wish to appear "cool" try to maintain the existence of a category of religious youth who are relatively less cool and more restrictively "religious" than they themselves are.[40]

In sum, most American teenagers live lives of cultural contestation, positioned between various cultural rubrics that compete for allegiance and are each associated with particular and meaningful social relationships, identities, and institutions. Most young people respond to this situation not by moving more fully into one or the other rubric, but by attempting to navigate a middle path between them. While such processes may sometimes seem frivolous and facile to outsiders, for the young people involved, these decisions carry potentially severe social consequences, since a misstep can result in a real sense of distance or alienation from an important peer group, a significant religious or ethnic identity or community, or even one's immediate family. In other words, at stake in these navigations is not simply a sense of temporary or surface-level teenage "identity," but deeply meaningful experiences and feelings of belonging, community, and selfhood. In order to respond to this situation, most American teenagers continually engage in strategic (though often not coherently logical or completely conscious) attempts to signify belonging to and identification with multiple locally salient social categories. The principal way they do this is through the subtle use of cultural materials, behaviors, and aesthetic genres as category symbols to signify multiple belonging and complex identities, as well as the strategic employment of discourses that portray more "traditional" behaviors as youthful and American, or vice versa. As will be seen throughout this book, the Muslim American teenagers studied here consistently revealed their deep similarity with other kinds of American teenagers both through their shared position within a situation of cultural contestation and through their use of strikingly similar solutions to the common and culturally complex adolescent American predicaments they faced.

Muslim Americans Managing Culturally Contested Lives

My three and a half years with a group of Muslim American young men ultimately led me to this finding: the central concerns and preoccupations of young urban American Muslim men are profoundly similar to those of most other American teenagers, focusing largely on coolness, pop culture, and fashion; girlfriends and romance; independence and pushing limits; and social acceptance, friendship, and family. The difference, however, lies in the fact that for the group of young men observed here, these concerns were continually intertwined with and sometimes experienced as being at odds with the expectations that surrounded being a "good Muslim" as defined by their local community. Consequently, when these young people were together, much of their time and attention was focused on figuring out how to resolve, or at least temporarily reconcile, the tensions that arose between these sets of cultural expectations. Explaining exactly how these young Muslims worked together to manage the cultural tensions present in their day-to-day teenage lives—in the areas of popular culture, communal obligation, romantic love, and public identity—and demonstrating how these efforts at cultural navigation marked Muslim youth as fundamentally similar to rather than inherently different from other American teenagers are the central aims of this ethnography. This book thus offers an ethnographically detailed and sociologically contextualized answer to the question that Muhammad posed to Yusef in the City Mosque's youth room one Sunday morning: "How are you an athlete, a math nerd, a rapper, a gangster, and an imam?" In other words, exactly *how* do you manage a culturally contested life?

2

"Cool Piety"

HOW TO LISTEN TO HIP HOP AS A GOOD MUSLIM

Friday Night at the Studio

It's a Friday night in early May and I'm lost. As I drive through dimly lit neighborhood streets bordering the highway, I'm trying to find an organization called FLA (Filipinos for Learning and Advancement), where tonight the Legendz are using a community recording studio to create backing tracks for a few of their own hip hop songs in preparation for an upcoming performance at Lakeview High School in Crestwood. Here on the West Side, the lack of adequate lighting makes it difficult to see street signs, so I slow down at each intersection to peer out my window. Complicating things further is the fact that many of the busier streets crossing the roads I'm on have no traffic signals, so driving across each intersection feels a bit risky. Finally, though, I see Mission Street and the parking lot that Muhammad described. I pull in, hop out of my car, and walk toward the only visible entrance—a single green door set back on the far left side of an otherwise nondescript, low-slung brick building with no visible windows. I knock hard three times and wait. Suddenly the door bursts open and light shines out from the interior into the parking lot. Muhammad, Abdul, and Yusef all greet me with "dap" handshakes and welcome me in.

"J.O.B.!" cries Muhammad, calling me by an abbreviated version of my name the boys sometimes used.

"Come check out the studio!" says Yusef.

They lead me down a brightly lit hallway lined with cubbies stuffed with kids' jackets and backpacks toward a door on the left. Abdul turns the knob and pushes it open, and we all follow him into a small but well-equipped recording studio with two large computer monitors, two computer keyboards, a music keyboard, and an old-looking green acoustic guitar leaning against the back wall. Three office-type swivel chairs face the computers. The boys all plop down in the chairs, and I grab a seat on a small stool behind them. At the far right end of the small rectangular room stands a tall, slim young man stationed behind a pair of turntables and wearing a set of large headphones. Dressed in a black baseball cap, an open button-down white shirt with an orange T-shirt underneath, and baggy tan pants, he seems a few years older than the Legendz, maybe in his early twenties. He looks Filipino.

Abdul says, "J.O.B., this is Steven, also known as DJ Prototype." Steven nods his head up toward me in acknowledgement, and I return the gesture.

"We're mixing down a song right now," says Yusef, "and then we can head out."

Steven shifts his headphones so they fit snugly on top of his head, cues up a beat, and performs some impressive scratching over the pulsing rhythm coming from the speakers and filling the room. The boys watch him with widening eyes as he finishes the song with a flourish of dynamic scratches on the turntable.

"Tight," Abdul says to him. "Now play the Roc Boys beat!" I recognize "Roc Boys" as the name of a recent Jay-Z song. Steven flips through some records in a crate, slides one out, lays it on the turntable, flips a switch, and lets it play. A driving, propulsive beat consisting of cracking snare drum and booming bass and punctuated by blasts of 1970s-style funk horns and clanging cowbells fills the air. The boys visibly brighten and nod their heads in sync with the rhythm.

Yusef, standing near Steven by the turntables, chants to the beat, "Put your middle fingers up to the cops! . . . Just kidding."

After the song fades, Muhammad tells me, "We're making a CD with all of our beats for the show because we can't take the speakers, and our *DJ here* can't make it." He says this last part with mock frustration and a sidelong glance at Steven, who smiles.

"Okay, y'all," Steven says, "this is the last track to mix." He turns his attention back to the bank of computers and the turntables. Another beat starts, and he performs some complicated scratching over it. As soon as he finishes the track, the boys respond with enthusiastic exclamations of "Aw yeah!" and "Tight!" and walk over to give him dap.

"Okay, you can keep your job!" Muhammad says. Steven's face breaks into a smile.

"That sounded great," I tell him, waiting at the end of the line for my turn to congratulate him.

Steven hands Yusef a CD with what I assume is a mix of the backing tracks. He then starts packing up the equipment, closing up the turntables into a case. The boys help him carry some of his gear out into the parking lot.

As we all walk toward Steven's white sedan, Abdul, half smiling, asks, "Why can't you come with us, you punk?"

Steven says, "I told you guys, I need to go to my grandmother's place tonight. She needs some help."

Muhammad says, "Okay, thanks," and then adds dramatically, with mock gravity, "And whatever you do, do it well, son." Steven smiles.

As we finish loading Steven's equipment into his car and he slams the trunk shut, Muhammad tells him, "Tell your grandmother we said hi, even though she doesn't know who we are."

"Yeah, tell her the Legendz say hi," Abdul adds. "And that we want her on a track. She'll be like, 'They want me on a what?'"

Steven smiles and says, "Okay, good luck tonight, y'all. I'll probably see you here next week." They all give him dap. He shuts his door and drives away.

———

Hip Hop and Urban American Social Assimilation

The small rectangular recording studio located inside the offices of Filipinos for Learning and Advancement as well as the adjacent recreational rooms designed for youth and teen activities served as a kind of "home away from the mosque" during the years I spent with the Legendz. On any given Friday or Saturday night, a few of the boys would meet up at "the studio" to work on tracks for their own songs or simply to play around and record silly improvised raps. This location was significant to the Legendz because it provided them with a space to create and work on their music. In the context of my ethnographic project, it was significant as well from a sociological perspective because it was one of the few spaces outside of school where the Legendz regularly socialized with non-Muslims. While they often ventured outside the mosque, their families' homes, and their neighborhoods—to bonfires at the beach, movies, or skateboard rides across town, for example—they generally did so in each other's company and in what was thus an exclusively Muslim friendship group. The group's activities related to hip hop music or performance were a notable exception to this pattern, as these events often involved the cultivation of friendships and social connections with non-Muslims.

The Legendz told me that it was their interest in recording their own hip hop songs that first led them to the FLA recording studio. By spending more time at the studio they had come to know Steven as well as DJ Dragnet, another young Filipino man who ran the organization. During the years I spent with them, the Legendz consistently collaborated with these DJs on recording projects and performances. The organization eventually asked Abdul and Muhammad to host "FLA Flows," its monthly open mic night for neighborhood youth, something that they continued to do for years.

Most of the Legendz's other friendships and acquaintances with non-Muslims were also oriented around a shared enthusiasm for hip hop music and culture. The friendship between Abdul and Muhammad and a neighborhood Vietnamese boy they called "T-Rex," for example, centered on recording goofy freestyle raps together as well as occasionally composing more serious hip hop pieces. Muhammad told me that after he informed his non-Muslim classmates at school that he was a rapper, they started listening to the Legendz's songs on MySpace and talked to him about his music and rapping. Abdul was asked to serve as the DJ for a school production that showcased the latest dancing trends of "jerking" and "shuffling"; Fuad performed in the same show as a dancer.

An interaction I witnessed between the Legendz and a Latino friend from Muhammad's school one night exemplified the way in which participation in hip hop culture could lead to recognition from non-Muslim peers. On that particular night, I attended a hip hop show with the Legendz at a downtown venue called the El Rey Theater. One of the group's friends was performing in the show. The crowd was a mix of hip, well-heeled young people of color and a smattering of white faces. As we walked toward the exit to get some fresh air during the intermission, Muhammad spied his friend Miguel across the room:

> Muhammad says, "I think I see someone from my school down there," looking down near the front of the stage. "I'm going to go talk to him." "OK," I say. He walks down the stairs towards the front of the stage. I see him greet and talk to a heavy-set Latino-looking kid in a blue hoodie. After a minute, he walks back up with his friend in tow, who he introduces to me as Miguel. The other boys greet this kid enthusiastically, giving him dap and saying, "What's up?!" Miguel says, "I was watching the show and I was like, 'Boo-ya! The Legendz should be up there!'" The boys kind of smile and look down shyly. "You guys would be perfect for this show!" Miguel says energetically. The boys smile and nod.

As can be seen in this exchange, as well as in the earlier episode with Steven the DJ, "hip hopper" was for the Legendz a widely recognized and desirable identity that could momentarily precede and eclipse that of "religious Muslim" in an interaction with non-Muslim peers. The commonly recognized tastes and practices of hip hop—dress, music, and slang—could provide a foundation for joint social recognition, shared activity, and friendship that could cut across social divisions of race, ethnicity, and religion that might otherwise have stymied the formation of such bonds.

In making meaningful social connections with other urban youth based on a shared engagement with hip hop culture, the Legendz were following a pattern observed by sociologists among other second-generation immigrants whose participation in hip hop music and style allowed them to gain acceptance and make social inroads among young people from outside their immediate ethnic community. When sociologists of immigration first considered the role of hip hop in assimilation in the 1990s, they primarily focused on arguing that involvement in African American–associated rap music and culture was connected with poor academic achievement and even "downward" economic trajectories, leading immigrant youth into what they called "segmented assimilation."[1] But these claims have been convincingly challenged by more recent studies, which have found no particular link between involvement in these cultural forms and low achievement or aspiration[2] and have also revealed that the great majority of second-generation immigrants—including many involved in hip hop music and style—do not experience downward generational mobility, but rather "horizontal mobility," a trajectory in which they take on occupations and therefore class positions similar to—not "below"—those of their parents.[3]

Instead of dwelling on the alleged connection between hip hop involvement and social mobility, more recent studies have focused on what seems to be the new normal: an urban America in which hip hop music *is* mainstream culture and hip hop fandom serves as a means of acceptance by and involvement with an increasingly multicultural urban youth population.[4] This use of hip hop as a basis for social connection with ethnic "others" has been seen at work among young West Indians, Haitians, and Mexicans in New York City; Vietnamese refugees in New Orleans; and Puerto Ricans in Yonkers, New

York.[5] Hip hop fandom and style can thus serve as mechanisms of social assimilation[6] into a wider urban American community. For the Legendz, this community included Filipinos at FLA, African Americans in their neighborhood, and Latinos at school.

Hip Hop and In-group Identity Generation

In addition to employing hip hop as a way to gain acceptance and make connections with a broader urban American community of non-Muslims, the Legendz also actively adapted the genre's music and culture in creative ways to develop their own *in-group* Muslim American identity and style. The resulting identity performance—which I call *cool piety*—tapped into broader African American urban cool while still exhibiting a close association with local standards of Islamic behavior to produce a nuanced and multifaceted presentation of Muslim American self. Cool piety was interactionally generated through the ongoing creative adaptation and deployment of hip hop music and culture among the members of the Legendz and their Muslim American peers. If hip hop fandom facilitated social assimilation into broader society by demonstrating to non-Muslims that one was adequately culturally American, it also facilitated the creation of a desirable Muslim American in-group identity by demonstrating *to other Muslim Americans and to oneself* that one was adequately culturally American while still paying heed to important local expectations for Islamic behavior and identity.

The Legendz's ability to demonstrate knowledge of and familiarity with hip hop music and culture increased their social status among their peers in the Muslim Youth Program. By displaying knowledge of African American and hip hop culture in front of other youth at the mosque (e.g., talking about Tupac Shakur, giving each other "dap" handshakes, reciting lyrics by Akon, T-Pain, and Busta Rhymes) and sharing their stories of life in working-class, urban neighborhoods (e.g., describing their experiences with drive-by shootings, narrow escapes from gang members, and drug sales at school), the Legendz worked to cultivate an aura of urban coolness among their generally more suburban peers. In turn, other mosque youth—and some youth group leaders—treated the boys as local experts on hip hop culture. On more than one occasion, I watched young women in the mosque approach the boys in a quiet corner at a youth group event and ask them to teach them a new dance that they had seen or heard about, such as "the Soulja Boy," "the jerk," or "the reject." Another time, I saw youth group member Aisha tap Yusef on the shoulder to tell him proudly, "I got tickets to the De La Soul show!" Similarly, youth group leaders Melvin and Hasan— both in their early twenties—regularly approached the Legendz and spoke to them about their own favorite hip hop artists, such as Kid Cudi, Mos Def, and the Wu Tang Clan.

The Legendz's attempts to draw on hip hop music and culture to contribute to and complicate their Muslim American identities faced a significant and practical challenge, however: the strong symbolic and cultural tension between much of popular hip hop music and local understandings of Islamic propriety. While neither the Legendz's parents nor the leaders of the City Mosque argued that all music was *haram* (religiously forbidden), they did openly disapprove of music that included references to (and could therefore be seen as encouraging) haram behaviors such as dancing, the use of alcohol or drugs, premarital sex, and the use of profane language. As one mosque leader told me, "*Halal* [permissible] music is halal. Haram music is haram." This local judgment cast much of mainstream hip hop, which frequently included references to and suggestions of haram topics, as outside the sphere of acceptability and presented the Legendz with a practical cultural dilemma: How could they be both involved hip hop fans—an identity central to their sense of urban American selfhood—and "good" practicing Muslims?

For the Legendz, the resolution to this dilemma lay in *how* they listened to the music. By engaging with hip hop music and culture in particular, strategic ways and adopting a local repertoire of "listening practices,"[7] the Legendz developed a way of being both acceptably Muslim and adequately hip hop by taking part in the ongoing identity performance of *cool piety*. While hip hop fandom in the service of social assimilation was oriented toward social integration into a broader urban community, the Legendz's use of hip hop listening practices to generate an aura of cool piety took place primarily within the in-group setting. Here, the boys cultivated and projected a sense of themselves as both religiously pious Muslims *and* cool urban American teenagers to each other, their Muslim American youth peers, and themselves.

Two important studies that convincingly demonstrate the central role of hip hop music and style in the development of Muslim American youth cultures were published as this book neared completion. Su'ad Abdul Khabeer's *Muslim Cool* and Hisham D. Aidi's *Rebel Music* use cultural history and targeted ethnography to elucidate the close and complex relationship between African American aesthetic forms and modern American Muslim youth identities, both immigrant and African American.[8] Like these books, this chapter considers the hip hop–influenced identity presentations of young Muslim Americans. My approach to understanding this cultural phenomenon differs slightly, however, in that my primary concern lies with revealing the routinized and interactional underpinnings of this particular Muslim American identity performance. Through a fine-grained analysis of interactions among the members of one small group of second-generation immigrant Muslim hip hop fans, this chapter identifies the particular and patterned micro-level processes out of which an identity performance of cool piety—which hinges on a careful balance between local standards of proper Islamic behavior and involvement in sometimes profane hip hop music and culture—is continually constructed and maintained in daily life.

The Listening Practices of the Legendz

Through a specific repertoire of three distinct listening practices, the Legendz managed to interact with Islamic and hip hop cultural structures and symbols in creative ways that generated an identity performance of cool piety. In the following sections, I outline these practices in detail and argue that such musical interactions constituted a central mechanism through which the Legendz engaged in the ongoing production of a certain version of Muslim American identity: the cool but pious Muslim.

ISLAMIC LISTENING: APPLYING RELIGIOUS RULES TO HIP HOP ENGAGEMENT

During the time I spent with the Legendz, they listened to, talked about, and informally performed songs by artists ranging from the sincere and "conscious" Black Star (rappers Mos Def and Talib Kweli) to the silly and "nasty" Sir Mix-a-Lot (of "Baby Got Back" fame). What the vast majority of the hip hop songs and artists in the Legendz's listening repertoire shared was the potential to present a lyric or sonic element that could be seen as conflicting with the local, normative expectations of good Islamic behavior. Although the Legendz themselves did not openly express a sense of conflict or dismay at their ability to simultaneously listen to such music and feel like appropriately religious Muslims, the frequent presence of others who might see these symbolic elements as conflicting meant that they needed to be continually aware of the *potential* for tensions between the content of hip hop and the moral standards of religious Islam to arise in their everyday lives.

In order to manage such cultural tensions, the Legendz invented and practiced modes of "Islamic listening," that is, ways of interacting with hip hop that adhered to local guidelines for appropriate Islamic behavior. I witnessed an instance of this kind of listening one Sunday afternoon in the main lobby of the mosque while Muhammad was speaking with Abshir and his cousin Sayed soon after the *Dhuhr* (midday) prayer. As the four of us stood near the front desk, the noisy bustle of parents and children spilling out of the adjacent prayer area surrounded us. Earlier, Muhammad had been telling the other two boys that he had some new hip hop by a Somali rapper on his MP3 player.

Muhammad lets Abshir listen through his earphones for a bit, and then passes them to Sayed. Sayed starts moving his body to the music. Muhammad reaches out both of his open hands towards Sayed, and in an exaggerated Arab accent, says, "Zere is no dancing in zee mosque, bruzzah [brother]." Sayed smiles and stops dancing, but keeps listening and bobbing his head slightly. Muhammad smiles.

In encouraging Sayed to stop dancing but allowing him to keep bobbing his head, Muhammad was promoting a specific way of listening to hip hop within the mosque, one that was less likely to clash with local Islamic behavioral standards. While the mosque location suggested a general standard of Islamic conduct, including a stance against dancing to music, its religious leaders—and Islamic theology, more broadly—provided no clear guidance regarding listening to popular music in an Islamically appropriate manner. The Legendz worked to fill this gap by providing themselves and their friends with ad hoc solutions to the problem of being a religious Muslim while listening to hip hop.

Two elements of Islamic listening, both of which are evident in the interaction between Muhammad and Sayed, demonstrate how this practice allowed the Legendz to feel that they were staying true to the fundamentals of Islamically appropriate behavior while also maintaining an identification with hip hop fandom. First, Islamic listening demanded an active engagement with norms of good Muslim behavior, as locally defined. Listening to hip hop within a setting governed by Islamic behavioral norms required the Legendz to proactively orient themselves as a certain kind of Muslim in relation to a cultural form with an officially indeterminate and troubled relationship with Islam, and to take a particular stance on that relationship. Expressing such a specific application of Islamic norms was what Muhammad did when he told Sayed, "There is no dancing in the mosque, brother" yet allowed him to continue to bob his head slightly. In this way, hip hop listening within Islamic communal settings became an occasion for the specific adaptation of Muslim modes of behavior to hip hop engagement, and vice versa. In practicing Islamic listening, the Legendz made their musical behavior—and themselves—into certain kinds of Muslims by aligning their embodied actions with local religious ideals. By listening to music in this way, the Legendz were actively practicing being a certain kind of "good Muslim" through a specific kind of engagement with hip hop.

A second element of this interaction demonstrates how this practice allowed the Legendz to identify as real hip hoppers even as they used religious rules to curtail their music listening. When practicing Islamic listening, the Legendz always made sure to signal their allegiance to youth culture in the course of the interaction. In this instance, Muhammad signified this identification with youth culture in two ways: by allowing Sayed to continue listening to the music and bobbing his head, and by parodying the accent of an Arab "mosque elder" while admonishing his friend. By enacting a comedic routine well known among mosque youth—a caricature of the overly serious and "uncool" mosque authority figure—Muhammad tried to portray himself as someone on hip hop's (and Sayed's) "side" even while actively restricting Sayed's hip hop behavior to align more closely with local religious expectations. In signifying allegiance to youth culture during the practice of Islamic listening, the Legendz thus worked to demonstrate—to each other, other youth, and themselves—that while they may have chosen to apply a religious norm in a particular case, they nonetheless maintained a youth-oriented perspective and were not utterly beholden to religious Islam.

The combination of applying and tailoring religious rules while signifying allegiance to youth culture allowed the Legendz to demonstrate their knowledge of and affinity for youth musical culture even as they worked to partially conform that culture to local Islamic standards. A second example of Islamic listening that occurred during and after a hip hop performance by the Legendz reinforces this point. In late summer of my first year with the Legendz, a group of college-aged Muslims who called themselves WeRyse and worked weekly with youth from the Muslim Youth Program organized a Muslim youth arts showcase. The final performance took place on a Saturday afternoon on a makeshift stage behind the mosque and was attended by about one hundred people, including some of the Legendz's families as well as the mosque's more youth-oriented leaders. On this occasion, the Legendz performed three numbers: a song about Muhammad's brothers, a political song about the stereotyping of Muslims after 9/11, and a song celebrating the Muslim Youth Program. As was always the case when the group performed for a Muslim-only or more general audience, the Legendz's songs were free of profane language or references to sex, drugs, or alcohol. Despite a few technical glitches in the course of their set (during one song, for example, the sound kept cutting in and out as a soundman frantically worked to resolve the situation), the Legendz were received warmly by the audience of youth, parents, and mosque leaders, who applauded heartily at the end of each number.

The morning following the performance, and after the normal Sunday youth group meeting, the Legendz gathered in the youth room with youth group leader Melvin to recount their performance of the previous day.

> Melvin says, "That sound was pretty messed up." Abdul says, "Yeah, because that guy had a soundboard from Toys R Us!" Everyone laughs. Melvin says, "I'm just glad none of you all was grabbing yourselves." Muhammad nods and says, "I was going like this." He takes his left hand and moves it down to his crotch but then passes it to the side. Melvin smiles.

Again, the two characteristic elements of "Islamic listening" are present in this interaction. First, during the show Muhammad was required to actively consider and apply a norm of Islamic behavior— bodily and sexual modesty—in order to make his cultural participation in hip hop compatible with his Islamic context. In this way, he was enacting a certain kind of Islamic behavior through the medium of hip hop, embodying Muslim moral standards through a familiar pop cultural form. Second, the day after the event Muhammad demonstrated to himself and others that he was aware of the (locally) un-Islamic gestures affiliated with hip hop, even if he chose not to use them. In telling the other Legendz that he did not grab his crotch, Muhammad let others know both that he had done the Islamically appropriate thing—that is, he had successfully tailored hip hop to an Islamic context—and that he *knew exactly what that un-Islamic thing was*. In particular, he demonstrated familiarity with a gesture of overt masculine sexuality drawn from hip hop culture while still revealing his commitment to Islamic norms by refusing to fully enact that gesture.

Another routinized form of Islamic listening that the Legendz engaged in was creating and performing Islamicized versions of popular rap and R&B songs. By changing the words to songs that they all knew had originally been "un-Islamic," the group kept its hip hop activity officially "Islamic" while at the same time allowing members to demonstrate to each other their familiarity with (often profane) urban hip hop culture. I witnessed the performance of one such parody on a late afternoon in a room at the back of the mosque, where the boys, who had only hours earlier attended a Qur'an lesson with Omar, were supposedly helping to clean up:

> I walk back into the social hall. I see Muhammad sweeping up with Fuad and Abdul standing nearby, towards the back of the room. It sounds as though the boys are singing a song. The tune seems familiar, but I can't figure out what it is. After a while, I realize that they're singing something to the tune of the new Snoop Dogg song "Sensual Seduction" but changing the words to "Spiritual Connection." Instead of repeating the song's highly sexual lyrics, they're singing about the mosque. Abdul, for example, sings, "Omar is talking about the Qur'an." Fitting their lyrics exactly into the meter of the song, they mimic the echo effect on the vocal of the original, singing, "Omar is talking about the Qur'an . . . Qur'an . . . Qur'aaaaan." They laugh a lot as they do this and start to perform a dance routine, with Muhammad holding his broom like a guitar. . . . They continue for another few minutes, dancing around and alternating between some of the sexual lyrics of the original ("I'm gonna take my time/She's gonna get hers before I get mine") and their own altered lyrics about the mosque ("We're going to go and pray to Allah . . . Allah . . . Allaaaaah").

These kinds of parodies—through which the Legendz could demonstrate their knowledge of both urban hip hop and Islamic religiosity—were common practice in the group and were often created together as a kind of game. One Saturday evening, I rode with

Muhammad, Tariq, Abdul, and their friend Hana as they picked up Muhammad's mother from her job at a local community-based organization. Muhammad was behind the wheel, and his mother sat in the passenger seat next to him. The radio was tuned to a popular hip hop and R&B station.

> A song comes on that everybody seems to know, and they're singing along. It's describing some kind of romantic situation. I later learn the song is called "Birthday Sex." As soon as the chorus enters, Muhammad turns down the volume to silence the second word, and in its place says "*Astaghfirullah*!" ("God forgive me!). So, in effect, the chorus sounds like this: "Birthday [Astaghfirullah!] . . . Birthday [Astaghfirullah!]." Hana laughs hard when Muhammad does this. When the chorus comes around again, Muhammad once more turns down the volume to silence the word "sex." From the back seat, Abdul sings different improvised words along with the chorus: "Birthday Text/Birthday Text/I'm gonna send my mom a Birthday Text."

During my time with the Legendz, the boys continually made slight adjustments to the practices of hip hop listening in order to fall more in line with Islamically appropriate behavior. They turned songs played on cell phones down or off at certain points to avoid obscene lyrics, edited and altered recited raps on the fly to remove or replace references to sex or drugs, and quelled overt dancing or other embodied responses to music within the mosque or other settings associated with Islamic normative behavior. In working to resolve such tensions between hip hop music and Islamic behavior—tensions that repeatedly emerged in the course of their daily lives—the Legendz were constantly pushed to openly consider and customize locally salient Islamic religious guidelines. In this way, the Legendz experienced what could be conceptualized as a fixed system of orthodox beliefs and practices as something immediately relevant and adaptable. By adapting their hip hop listening to Islamic religious practice, and vice versa, the boys maintained a familiarity with "Islam" as something real, lived, and accommodating. For the Legendz, the musical practice of Islamic listening was a local means of producing a dynamic religious identity and a way of experiencing Islam that was creative, fun, and compatible with urban American youth culture.

In consistently working to interact with hip hop music and culture in ways that nonetheless allowed members to position themselves as "good Muslims," the Legendz engaged in a local Muslim American version of a process that sociologist Prudence Carter terms "cultural straddling,"[9] a strategy that has also been recognized among African American and Latino youth in public schools as well as among highly religious Christian and Jewish young people. Like the Legendz, these young people make careful and strategic adjustments to their engagements with particular youth-associated cultural practices— such as listening to popular music (but turning down inappropriate songs), dressing in a "ghetto" style (but moderating such clothing's bagginess), using slang and curse words (but not in front of adults), consuming "worldly" fashion (but amending it to be more modest), and attending parties (but resisting drugs and alcohol).[10] In these ways, youth living culturally contested lives work to participate in teenage social activities in ways that emphasize their compatibility with community- and adult-approved behavior while also signaling their youthful coolness. Like the Legendz, other young American cultural straddlers seek to be both "good" and "cool" and utilize particular interactions with youth cultural behaviors, symbols, and activities in their attempts to strike this balance.

LISTENING LIKE A COOL MUSLIM: FINDING ISLAMIC PIETY IN HIP HOP

A second way in which the Legendz experienced Islamic belonging in conjunction with their hip hop affiliation was by finding Islam *within* the wider genre of hip hop, or, more specifically, by collaboratively locating elements expressive of Muslim religiosity in more broadly popular rap songs. American hip hop is uniquely suited for this purpose. Due to the deep historical links between many urban African American communities and Islam, a sizable number of African American rap artists either are Muslim themselves or at least have a familiarity with Muslim ideas and culture.[11] Many prominent Muslim rappers are or were at one time members of the Five-Percent Nation, a breakaway sect of the Nation of Islam.[12] The presence of Five Percenter, Sunni, and Sufi Muslims—as well as those familiar with these sects—within hip hop means that many well known hip hop songs are inflected with phrases from Islamic scripture, Arabic-sounding musical cues, or other Muslim-associated cultural elements that are often overlooked by the casual listener.[13] The Legendz's active engagement with these Islamic elements in hip hop, expressed through their practice of "listening like cool Muslims," granted a powerful local resonance to this music.

I first witnessed this listening practice on a fall afternoon during a trip to Burger King with Muhammad, Abdul, and Fuad. After the regular Sunday youth program meeting let out, the four of us walked out of the mosque together and talked about getting something to eat. After some debate between Abdul and Fuad over which fast food place—Little Caesars Pizza or Burger King—would provide the most food for the least amount of money, Abdul's reminder that Burger King had a dollar menu settled the question. The four of us wandered slowly across the street, making our way around the side of the building and then in through the side door of the relatively empty Burger King. After selecting from the dollar menu and getting our food, we filled our large cups with ice and soda and sat down at a table by the wall opposite the door through which we had entered. That day our lunchtime conversation wended its way through some of the usual topics—better and worse teachers at school, shows to watch on the Disney Channel, upcoming social plans with families—and some less common ones—Abdul's mother's recent trouble with her immigration status—before settling into the familiar topic of hip hop. Muhammad spoke about the kind of raps his brother was writing, Abdul and Muhammad described their ideas for new songs, and all three discussed a show they had played a few weeks earlier. Eventually Muhammad brought up the recent Hip Hop Awards that had been televised on Black Entertainment Television (BET). This led to a spirited debate on the "top MCs" (rappers) of all time, with contenders such as Jay-Z, Common, Tupac Shakur, and Kanye West.

As we walked out the door and turned the corner of the building back onto Jayne Street, this exchange took place:

> Abdul says, "Talib Kweli is one of my favorites. He's good." I say, "I saw Mos Def and Talib Kweli perform one time as Black Star." "Really?" Abdul and Muhammad say, with excitement. Muhammad asks, "What songs did they do?" I say, "I can't really remember. . . . It was a while ago." Abdul asks, "Did they do that song 'Definition'?" I say, "I'm not sure. . . . They did the one about, 'Black is the . . .'" Muhammad picks up the line and starts reciting the rap: "Black is the color of my true love's hair . . ." Muhammad, Abdul, and Fuad are all now rapping together: "Black is the veil that the *Musliminas* wear!" "That's tight!" Abdul says.

Here, the Legendz were enjoying music and each other's company through shared musical engagement. By doing so, they were also experiencing a common social identity. Since identity can be both an emotional and a sensory experience, music—particularly when inflected with identity symbols and listened to in a coordinated manner—is an especially powerful means of producing experiences that allow for identification with others.[14] The identity group–building function of listening to music can be seen here in the active and shared process of locating and celebrating Islamic cues in the music.

More than merely gaining a sense of "Muslimness" by listening to music together—something that members of any religious group can do with sacred or sacralized music—the Legendz in this and other situations worked to pinpoint and celebrate a certain kind of Muslimness located within a certain kind of music. The specific symbols of Islam identified and celebrated by the Legendz when they listened to hip hop were almost always resonant of a *high level* of Islamic piety. In the previous example, the lyric that the Legendz jointly latched onto describes a Muslim woman ("Muslimina") wearing the hijab, or headscarf ("the veil"), understood within Islam as a sign of religious devotion. The color of the veil—black—deepened this association with piety, as a black hijab denotes an especially strong commitment to modesty.

When the symbol of the black hijab was invoked by popular rapper Mos Def and then recited by the boys, their response was enthusiastic ("That's tight!"). In contrast, the sight of a woman such as one of their mothers or sisters wearing a hijab at home or within the mosque community never elicited this kind of energetic approval. This symbol of Islamic piety was jointly celebrated by the Legendz in this instance because it was framed by a musical context associated with youth, coolness, and an extrareligious worldliness. Most of the lyrics in this Black Star song and others to which the Legendz listened in this way are *not* primarily or centrally concerned with Islam but rather insert religious symbols into a diverse array of lyrical themes and topics, including romantic encounters, neighborhood affiliations, and African American identity. As a result, the Islamic elements within these songs never become all encompassing, and the strong beats and dance-associated rhythms pull against an overarching sense of Islamic propriety. The rap songs in which the Legendz located Islamic symbols always possessed two qualities: lyrics or musical cues denoting a high degree of piety (e.g., the call to prayer, Qur'anic scripture or characters, the hijab) and a musical and lyrical context surrounding these symbols that was unmistakably hip hop and associated with American—and often African American—youth culture.

An alternate interpretation of the Legendz's celebration of Islamic symbols in popular hip hop music could be that it was *not* about manifesting a blend of grounded Muslim belonging and dynamic coolness, but rather about the boys recognizing their own religious identity within mainstream hip hop. It is true that the multicultural roots, increasing diversity, and overwhelming popularity of hip hop music make it possible for young people from a range of ethnic and religious backgrounds to "find" references to their own identity nested within contemporary hip hop music.[15] However, my years of observing the Legendz revealed that there was more than a simple recognition of their identity going on when they listened for Islamic cues in hip hop. First, the Legendz did not deem the appearance of *any* kind of Muslim identity or Islamic reference in popular hip hop as worthy of enthusiasm—only those that were clearly highly pious, even within an otherwise non-Islamic musical framework. In fact, the Legendz frequently accused popular rappers who dropped Islamic references into their songs or self-presentation too casually of not being "real" Muslims and being "just" Five Percenters. Part of the conversation in Burger King had taken up this very issue:

> "So Talib Kweli is Muslim?" I ask. "Yeah," they say. Abdul says, "Mos Def and Talib Kweli are both Muslim." Muhammad says, "And not Five Percenters either." Abdul, apparently mishearing, asks, "They're Five Percenters?" "No," says Muhammad, emphasizing the next point, "They're *not* Five Percenters." "Is Tribe Called Quest Muslim?" Muhammad asks. "Q-Tip is," says Abdul. "Oh yeah," Muhammad says. "I think he had an Allah chain on. . . . Some Muslim rappers, when they win an award, they just say, 'I want to thank God.' When Mos Def gets up there, he says, 'I want to thank Allah!'" Muhammad holds his arms dramatically above him as he says this. "And he talks about the Prophet Muhammad (Peace Be Upon Him) and the Qur'an and all this stuff. . . . But some rappers just wear Allah chains. . . . T-Pain is Muslim." Abdul says, "Akon is Muslim." Fuad says, "That's why in that song 'Bartender' he says, 'I don't smoke/I don't drink.'" Abdul nods.

While hip hoppers who made reference to Islam in their songs provided the Legendz with opportunities to be cool Muslim listeners, those who did so without proving religious devotion in other ways were treated with suspicion. The songs of the latter type of rappers were not celebrated or used as material for meaningful listening in the same way. At the other end of the spectrum—as will be explored further later—devout Muslim rappers who were considered primarily Islamic but had achieved some level of mainstream pop success, such as the groups Native Deen and Outlandish, were regarded as "too religious" and not cool. Therefore, it was not the mere appearance of *any* sign of Muslim identity in rap music that gained the Legendz's approval, but rather instances of deep Islamic piety nested within a primarily nonreligious hip hop framework. It was this kind of Islamic listening that was preferred by the Legendz, because locating highly Islamic symbols within popular, cool, and sometimes profane hip hop songs allowed the group to demonstrate an allegiance to Islamic piety without seeming overly devout.

RESISTING THE "TOO RELIGIOUS"

Sociologists who study religious youth in the United States have found that most practicing young people are wary of being identified as or associated with those whom they consider "too religious," that is, those whose behavior and attitude suggests an overly serious religiosity and the prioritization of piety over all else.[16] The Legendz's behavior was consistent with this finding. The boys regularly poked fun at people whom they considered religious in an all-encompassing way, such as mosque adults who lectured youth on the minutiae of Islamic rules or youth who spent the bulk of their time praying or memorizing the Qur'an. In this way, the boys engaged in a kind of boundary work similar to that employed by the white evangelical Christian college and high school students studied by Amy Wilkins and Alan Peshkin, respectively, who often drew attention to other, more "boring" and "pious" Christian young people in order to position themselves as more "cool" or "interesting" in comparison.[17] When it came to criticizing the overly religious, the Legendz most frequently targeted Muslim musicians and rappers who limited themselves to addressing solely Islamic themes. Whenever I accompanied the boys to concerts by Muslim musicians, I saw them repeatedly poke fun at performers whose strictly Islamic lyrics or self-presentation made them seem "boring," "cheesy," or, from the Legendz's perspective, out of touch with the "real" world. This was exactly how Muhammad characterized Muslim musicians one day at a community concert when I asked the boys whether they would consider giving one of their rap demo CDs to the popular Muslim musician Sami Yusuf:

> I overhear Muhammad talking to Yassir about a song they are working on called "This Is How We Pray." "Hey," I say to Muhammad and the others. "You should give Sami Yusuf a demo." "Man, what's he gonna do?" says Muhammad. "He probably can't

get us on his label. . . . We'll probably give it to him and he'll say (affecting accent and raising his arms upward with palms facing each other about shoulder's width apart): 'My label is Allah.'" The other guys laugh.

In contrast to their celebration of rappers who injected signs of Islamic piety into broadly popular hip hop, the Legendz were disparaging of Muslim musicians whose music was primarily about Islam. In listening to more popular hip hop and identifying symbols of Islamic piety within it, the boys were simultaneously able to express connection with Islamic devotion and signal urban American cool—a specific experience and expression of identity that listening to overtly "Muslim" rap did not afford them.

By repeatedly listening to hip hop in a way that involved a constant search for messages of Islamic piety within a popular audio landscape, the boys experienced and presented themselves as certain kinds of Muslims, those who could and did establish a connection to religious piety and youthful worldliness at the same time, that is, those who demonstrated a *cool piety*. While the occurrence of Muslim religious symbols within popular music provided an opportunity for the Legendz to experience cool piety through hip hop, it was through the *process* of actively locating and sharing this particular expression of Islamic American symbolism that the Legendz repeatedly cast themselves and each other as cool Muslim Americans. I witnessed another instance of this kind of collaborative identity expression one evening when my wife, Saba, and I accompanied the Legendz to a dinner event at the mosque during which we discussed hip hop.

> As we sit at the table with the Legendz, Yusef tells Saba about the performance the boys had earlier in the evening. Saba tells him, "We just got the new Lupe Fiasco CD. Have you heard it?" He smiles and nods enthusiastically. "That's a really good CD! I think he actually has the *adhan* (call to prayer) on one of the tracks!" Saba and I nod.

This exchange once again demonstrates that symbols of devout Islamic practice—here, the call to prayer—were what attracted the Legendz's special attention whenever they listened to popular hip hop as cool Muslims. While it is possible that Yusef noticed the call to prayer while listening to this CD on his own, his uncertain phrasing ("I *think* he actually has . . .") suggests that he may have heard this piece of information from another Muslim friend. This possibility, as well as the way in which he excitedly passed the news on to us, demonstrates how the practice of listening to hip hop as a cool Muslim was a *social* experience, one granted meaning through interaction. When Yusef told us that he believed that this popular hip hop album included a symbol of Islamic piety, he went beyond celebrating a reference to his own minority religion within a pop cultural form to show us that he was someone who was able to identify—and who identified with— this particular combination of Islamic and urban American musical symbols. In other words, he was a cool, pious Muslim.

PIVOTING AWAY FROM PIETY: USING HIP HOP TO SIGNIFY A COMPLICATED MUSLIM IDENTITY

While the Legendz sometimes interacted with hip hop in ways meant to emphasize a simultaneity of Islamic piety and pop cultural cool, at other times they used hip hop to briefly but intentionally suggest their familiarity with behavioral elements of hip hop culture that were deemed un-Islamic by most of their community. In so doing, they worked to complicate their own Muslim identities by employing hip hop's haram content to symbolically "pivot away" from Islam and project a degree of independence from the religion's norms. As discussed earlier, the Legendz's ability to present a multidimensional identity and signal extra-Islamic worldliness through participation in hip hop was important to them because they, like most religious youth in the United States, were wary of those whom they considered "too religious." One way the Legendz distinguished themselves from those whom they perceived to be overly devout Muslims was through the strategic deployment of hip hop's un-Islamic content in everyday interactions with other young Muslims.

The broad popularity of mainstream hip hop among mosque youth and its well-known association with deviant themes made it a particularly useful resource for the Legendz's occasional presentation of a less than devout Islamic identity to each other and their Muslim peers. Since popular hip hop songs and rappers were so familiar to youth in the mosque and the association between mainstream hip hop and deviant (and un-Islamic) behavior was so strong, the Legendz needed only to make the slightest suggestion of affiliation with popular (and profane) hip hop to gain a certain countercultural cachet. An incident that took place one afternoon during a youth program meeting at the mosque demonstrates just how subtle these implications of deviance from Islamic behavior could be. During this session, the Legendz were asked to prepare a rap song for an upcoming youth program reunion. As they worked on the song, the boys considered various currently popular rap songs as templates.

> The crew of boys gathers to start working on their song. I sit with them. They joke around for a while, then Muhammad takes the lead. "OK," he asks the group. "What beats can we use?" People throw out ideas—Tupac, Timbaland, but nothing seems to stick. . . . They play around with different rhymes set to songs they know, trying to get some good lines for their song for the reunion. Once in a while Abdul does a line in a heavy Arab accent. After Muhammad tries one line out, Yusef says, "Yeah, you could use that!" Muhammad continues rapping: "MYP is my other half/ Lean like a cholo. . . . Lean like a Muslim." People in earshot laugh, especially the girls at the table working on the picture collages. Muhammad smiles.

In this incident, Muhammad improvised a brief parody of the then-popular hip-hop song "Lean Like a Cholo" by the rapper Down AKA Kilo. Through his recitation—and adaptation—of a portion of the song, Muhammad called to mind the lyrical content of the well-known original, which focuses on gang lifestyles, casual sex, and dancing. It was the juxtaposition of these un-Islamic themes with the mosque location and the word "Muslim" that made Muhammad's parody funny and caused the nearby girls to laugh. By making a fleeting reference to this song and its content, Muhammad evoked a symbolic distance between himself and orthodox Islamic behavior, interactively suggesting that he and the other Legendz were familiar with such songs, lyrics, and perhaps even the behavior they described. In this way, the strategic use of hip hop symbolism complicated the group's Muslim identity, making them seem and feel that they were more than merely good Muslims, even if most of their behavior still hewed closely to local Islamic norms.

In such cases, the Legendz's interactional suggestions of deviance were not simply a matter of ignoring appropriate Islamic behavior and using hip hop profanity. They involved an active "pushing off" against Muslim behavioral norms through the use of specific Islamic practices and references as more "conservative" foils for their brief displays of hip hop–inflected deviance. This practice was illustrated by several interactions I witnessed among group members. One morning as the Legendz were working together to prepare a presentation on the duties of a good Muslim for the youth group, Fuad intentionally misheard the name of the revered scholar al-Bukhari as "Bacardi," the brand of rum frequently referenced by mainstream rappers. On another occasion, after sitting through a lecture on the *seerah* (the life of the Prophet Muhammad), Abshir altered the Arabic word to "Serena," which triggered a group recitation of an explicitly sexual verse in the Kanye West single "Gold Digger." And, during a humorous hypothetical conversation on how one might pray in a nightclub, Yusef modified prayer gestures to suggest a funky new dance move but, recalling that he was in the mosque, quickly stopped himself. Such hip hop–associated touches of haram behavior among the Legendz were nearly always brief and made in close proximity to Islamic symbols or practices. Usually they also involved stifled laughter and knowing glances—signals to each other and to anyone watching them that though they might be good Muslims, they knew about more than just Islam.

The Legendz's interactional attempts to distinguish themselves from musicians who hewed strictly to Islamic themes, as described earlier, was another way in which they used hip hop's association with deviance to pivot away from what they considered an all-encompassing and monochromatic religious identity. This form of distancing was even more precise, as through it the Legendz "pushed off" not only against Islamic rules in general, but also against attempts by adult Muslim leaders and musicians to combine forms of hip hop culture and Islamic religiosity to appeal to youth. Although the Legendz were practicing Muslims involved in hip hop, they resisted being pigeonholed as "Muslim rappers" because to them this identification signified a boring, overly serious, and one-dimensional identity. Abdul demonstrated such a resistance to the "Muslim rapper" label one day as we ate lunch with the other Legendz at a local fast food restaurant. Toward the end of the meal, I asked Abdul whether the boys were "Muslim rappers."

> There's a pause. Abdul says, "I mean, we are . . . but only when we're playing for Muslim things." "So you guys only play Muslim stuff when you're playing for Muslim audiences?" I ask. "No," he says. "I mean, we play political stuff . . . and we talk about Islam and everything. But my other stuff that I write, I mean, it's crazy. You wouldn't want to see it."

In distancing himself from a strictly religious identity, even that of a "Muslim rapper," Abdul used the association of hip hop with deviance to suggest a more dangerous side to his identity, one that was so "crazy" that I "wouldn't want to see it." By employing hip hop in this way, Abdul and the other Legendz repeatedly insinuated that their identity included a potentially un-Islamic dimension—one that existed just out of sight—without actually needing to engage in haram behavior. Such visible hip hop associations signaled a degree of cultural autonomy and projected a cool, complicated, and more mysterious Muslim identity to themselves and others.

There is nothing surprising about young people engaging in cultural practices that push the boundaries of adult or communal acceptability. Teenagers are known for participating in fashion, music, and social behavior that intentionally "pushes the buttons" of their parents and other adults in their social environments.[18] Sometimes this behavior is interpreted by adults as more threatening than it actually is, and sometimes it does in fact correlate with "deviant" and dangerous behavior. But for most young people who, like the Legendz, are situated between competing cultural rubrics of cool, youthful cultural expectations on the one hand and more responsible, adult-approved behavior on the other, involvement in deviance-associated youth behaviors is primarily a *symbolic* and *strategic* act. Young people mobilize category symbols (e.g., music, fashion, language, physical affect) associated with recognizable youthful styles like ghetto, goth, street, and gangsta in ways that demonstrate their allegiance with such rubrics without necessitating actual involvement in the deviant behaviors commonly associated with these styles. In this way, young people caught between cultural expectations of "good" and "cool"—African American youth from "decent" or middle-class families, second-generation immigrants with familial expectations for success, white middle-class college students flirting with goth styles, and evangelical Christians living on college campuses[19]—can present a more general, worldly, and urban coolness, often primarily *to each other*, while maintaining legitimate membership in their particular "traditional" communities.

Conclusion

This chapter has demonstrated two ways in which the Legendz engaged with hip hop music and culture to manage the cultural dilemma of being both practicing Muslims and urban American teenagers. First, their engagement with hip hop brought them into social contact with non-Muslim youth and therefore enmeshed them more deeply in an ethnically diverse urban American community. Using Herbert Gans's helpful formulation, this use of hip hop for the presentation of a culturally American self to non-Muslim outsiders led to further social "assimilation" into the broader city.[20] Second, and more central to my analysis, the Legendz creatively used the cultural materials of hip hop music and style to develop a sufficiently Islamic yet effectively cool identity performance among themselves, that is, *within and primarily for the in-group*. They thus developed particular practices—Islamic listening, listening like a cool Muslim, and pivoting away from piety—to infuse their communal Muslim selves with American pop cultural styles, behaviors, and references.

To use Gans's distinction, the focus of this in-group process was "acculturation"—becoming more culturally American through adaptations to the in-group culture within and for the group itself.[21] Through their ongoing listening practices, the Legendz incubated an innovative and dynamic form of multicultural Muslim American youth identity that I call *cool piety.*

Recent scholarship has emphasized the role of hip hop music and culture in allowing urban youth of various backgrounds to find common tastes and join a "multiethnic mainstream."[22] I agree with this claim and watched this process take place among the Legendz. But focusing mainly on the intergroup aspect of hip hop can overlook the ways in which hip hop can also be used on the *intra-group* level to reinforce a local, communal, tightly knit ethnic identity by infusing it with an attractive vitality and association with a broader urban and African American–associated style of "cool." The explosion of hip hop's popularity since the mid-1990s has meant that the music and style are now available through mass media to a wide range of individuals and communities, including those with no physical proximity to African Americans or even America.[23] This widespread consumption of hip hop, in tandem with its aesthetic flexibility and adaptability,[24] means that the music can be taken up in a variety of social contexts in ways that allow members of specific bounded racial, religious, or ethnic communities to engage in local versions of the particular listening practices outlined in this chapter—listening to the music in a way that feels compatible with their in-group behavioral norms, seeking and experiencing links between their own specific identities and broader hip hop culture, and complicating their potentially monochromatic identities with a sense of urban American cool. Together, these listening practices can contribute to the incubation of a sense of locally loyal yet culturally mainstream identity, experienced primarily within the in-group setting. This chapter has demonstrated a Muslim American version of this process and shown how, for the Legendz, hip hop music and its associated listening practices served as crucial elements in making young Muslims in America feel like young Muslim Americans.

3

"The American Prayer"

ISLAMIC OBLIGATION AND DISCURSIVE INDIVIDUALISM

The American Prayer

It's late Sunday afternoon at the City Mosque and as I reach the bottom of the front staircase and head into the lobby, I nearly run smack into Abshir, who is quickly approaching me with what seems like a pressing question.

"John," he asks me excitedly, "can you give us a ride to Metro Sports? We need to get some screws to fix the basketball hoop." He points to Fuad, standing next to him, who is holding the rim and net, which are detached from the backboard. "See?" he says.

"Sure," I say, "I can take you guys."

"Okay, let's go!" says Abshir, who turns and leads the four of us—Abdul, Muhammad, Fuad, and me—back through the lobby, snaking through a crowd of children gathered in the social hall for what seems like a birthday party and out the back door into the rear parking lot.

"My car's over there," I tell the guys, pointing toward my silver Honda Accord, parked in the lot's back corner. Just as we start walking across the lot, a dark green Infiniti crosses in front of us and slows to a stop, cutting off our path forward. Through the window, I recognize the driver as Abshir's father, who works as a security guard in a building nearby.

Abshir steps up to the car as his father rolls down the window. After a brief wave to Fuad, Abdul, and me, Abshir's father says something softly to him in Arabic. Abshir turns back to the three of us and asks me, "John, do you know what time *Asr* (afternoon) prayer is today?"

I shake my head no: "Sorry, I don't."

Muhammad turns toward the back of the mosque and sees Yusef standing by the door. He yells over to him, "Hey, Yusef! What time is Asr?"

Under his breath, so that we can hear but his father cannot, Abshir whispers a quiet plea directed at Yusef: "Say that it's later . . ."

Yusef calls back cheerfully, "It's about to start in a few minutes!"

Abshir's face falls as Muhammad relays this information to Abshir's father, still seated in the car: "Abu Abshir, Asr will start in a few minutes."

Abshir's father nods. His son is crestfallen, as his trip to Metro Sports has been forestalled by the timing of the prayer. We all turn around and walk back toward the mosque, Abshir dragging his heels, slowly bringing up the rear.

We walk through the social hall and meander toward the prayer area, stopping at the front desk to hang out and joke with Hamed, who is working there today. After a few minutes, I notice Abshir's father walk into the prayer area, followed by a few other men.

"Are you guys ready to pray?" Yusef asks us, walking into the lobby.

We all take off our shoes, step into the prayer area, and sit on the green carpet, waiting for the prayer to start. Across from us, near the southeast corner, we hear Abshir's father's voice—"*Allahu Akbar* (God is great)! Allahu Akbar!"—and I look over to see him engaged in the motions of prayer. The boys look confused, as it seems as though Abshir's father has begun the Asr prayer, which is supposed to be done with others, even though people have not yet congregated.

Abdul shrugs and says to the rest of us, "I guess we're praying by ourselves . . . so let's just pray by ourselves. Here, let's pray here."

We all line up in a little group—Abdul in front, and me, Muhammad, Fuad, Yusef, and Abshir in the row behind—and Abdul leads the prayer. When we finish, we hear some murmuring from a group of older men now gathered near the southeast corner of the prayer area with Abshir's father.

I look up to see Abshir's father striding toward us, speaking quickly in Arabic, his brow furrowed with frustration. Abshir interprets for him, saying to us, "He said it's the American prayer."

His father, now standing directly in front of us, says in English with growing irritation, "Why did you not wait?"

Another man behind him adds in a similarly aggravated tone, "Now we cannot pray all together."

"We heard him say 'Allahu Akbar,' so we thought we were praying on our own," Abdul says by way of explanation. Most of the older men shake their heads in apparent disapproval.

Muhammad says in a defensive tone: "It was just a misunderstanding." Yusef steps between Muhammad and the older men as if to defuse the tension between the two groups.

The older men walk to the other side of the room to start their prayer. The boys seem unsure whether to stay and pray again or not. One of the older men, who appears to be South Asian, says to them with a touch of resignation, "You can go. You have already prayed."

We walk out into the main lobby and then turn into the side office, where Muhammad and a few other boys start talking, apparently about this idea of the "American prayer," to Ibrahim, an Indian man who works there. Muhammad asks him, "If it's not an American mosque, then why is there an American flag out front?"

"Yeah," Fuad replies.

Ibrahim says, calmly, "Yes, but that is outside the mosque. We are inside the mosque; it is different."

Muhammad looks over at the wall, where a list of health regulations for workers under state law is posted. "What about this?" he says. "Why do you have a state law thing on your wall?"

Ibrahim says, "That's for employees."

We walk back out into the lobby. Abshir grumbles, "He always says that, about the American prayer."

I lean over toward Muhammad and ask him, "What's this American prayer thing?"

"Oh," Muhammad says. "Abshir's father was saying that when people pray on their own, that's the American way of praying. But we should be praying as a group."

———

This episode highlights a significant and central cultural tension that existed within the City Mosque and in the everyday lives of the Legendz and their Muslim friends. On the one hand, as practicing Muslims, the Legendz were part of a religious tradition that even in its more liberal manifestations involves some degree of deference to externally imposed commitments and obligations.[1] This aspect of their daily lives can be seen here in the call to prayer, which signals to practicing Muslims that—whether they feel like it or not—they are expected by God as well as fellow community members to stop all other activities and fulfill one of the core requirements of their religion, daily salat (prayer). On the other hand, the Legendz were also young people brought up in America who had been inculcated with American notions of the self—particularly the idea that each individual should possess a strong sense of autonomy or freedom from social influence.[2] This aspect of their daily lives could be seen in their enthusiasm for pursuing their personal interests and endeavors when and as they desired, such as by going to a sports store one moment, skateboarding the next, and later driving to a fast food restaurant or going to the beach. Almost as important to American teenagers as their ability to do what they want when they want is the *appearance* that they have this autonomy over their actions.[3] In addition, young people in the United States are generally expected to present themselves as possessing two other qualities associated with modern American individualism—agency, or individually driven effort,[4] and reflexivity, the ability to "step back" and reflect on one's own social position.[5]

An ongoing dilemma faced by the Legendz was how to participate in their Islamic religious life—a life structured in part around external authority, sacred obligation, and communal requirement—while preserving a sense of themselves as culturally American teenagers expected to act autonomously, demonstrate individual agency, and possess a reflexive stance on the world. This chapter shows how the Legendz dealt with this cultural dilemma by engaging in the forms and rituals of religious Islam while using particular linguistic and embodied strategies meant to bring a sense of autonomy, agency, and reflexivity to these communally rooted and theologically obligatory endeavors. Through repeated and patterned practices that involved participation in Islamic ritual but also utilized discourses resonant with meanings of American individualism, the Legendz and their friends worked to interactively construct an Islamic life that could be experienced as consistent with contemporary American cultural expectations of personal autonomy, individual agency, and critical self-reflexivity while simultaneously meeting obligatory and often personally meaningful religious requirements.

In this chapter, I identify three specific practices though which the Legendz sought to claim this elusive cultural middle ground by symbolically encasing their Islamic activities in forms of discursive individualism. First, they demonstrated autonomy in religious action by exhibiting a measure of visible control over the specific ways in which they fulfilled Islamic ritual, especially in terms of the starting times of their daily prayers. Second, the boys strategically evoked the specter of an imagined "extreme Muslim" while together in order to portray themselves and each other as self-reflexive and freethinking young Muslims. Finally, they consistently talked about their fulfillment of locally normative religious action in language that emphasized the importance of their own agency or individual efforts. Together, these practices contributed to the Legendz's ongoing strategic efforts to live out an externally authoritative Islamic ethic in a way that was consonant with modern American cultural expectations of autonomy, agency, and reflexivity.

Autonomy in Religious Action:
Controlling the When of One's Prayer

This chapter's opening vignette offers two visible instances in which the cultural expectations of externally imposed religious and communal authority came into conflict with the American teenage priorities of personal autonomy and individual agency. The first tension emerged when Abshir's desire to go to the sports store—to do what *he* wanted to do with his friends—ran up against the externally imposed and socially reinforced ritual obligation of afternoon prayer. This led to Abshir's disappointment, as his immediate individual and youthful desires were eclipsed by a locally powerful communal and religious expectation. The second, more dramatic, visible tension arose when the Legendz began reciting a congregational prayer before and separately from the adults in the mosque's prayer area. Responding to this, Abshir's father articulated an opinion echoed by other parents of second-generation immigrants in the United States, namely, that the youth were becoming more "American" and that this change was observable in, and equivalent to, their more individualistic behavior.[6] The Legendz's defense of their earlier and separate prayer, and even of the label "American" and state laws, reflected their openness to modes of prayer that were more in line with their sense of being Americans, residents of a US state, and young people. Although the "American prayer" incident was unusual in the way that cultural conflict between communal obligation and individual action was made so clearly visible, this episode also hinged on what turned out to be a consistent site of subtle cultural contestation for the Legendz over the years I spent with them: the starting time of daily prayers.

In the City Mosque, there was no more direct or frequent expression of religious obligation than the call to prayer (adhan), which could be heard throughout the building five times a day. Most frequently delivered by Salman's father and taught to the Legendz by Omar during my time in the community, the call to prayer is a melodic, vocally drawn-out, two- to five-minute exhortation in Arabic to Muslims within earshot to come to prayer. It begins with *"Allaaaaaaaaaa-hu Akbar! Allaaaaaaaaaa-hu Akbar!"* ("God Is the Greatest") and then goes on to entreat those within hearing distance: *"Hayya'alas-salah! Hayya'alas-salah!"* ("Hurry to prayer!") Because the Legendz and other teenagers in the Muslim Youth Program were most often in the mosque for Sunday morning meetings, the most relevant call to prayer for this group came at midday, or Dhuhr prayer, which usually took place around 1 or 1:30 p.m. While Sunday Dhuhr prayer was not regarded as the most theologically important group prayer by members of the City Mosque (that would have been the congregational *Jummah* prayer on Fridays), it was a socially meaningful prayer in the community because of the large number of people present in the mosque on Sunday afternoons for classes, social gatherings, and volunteer opportunities. This heavy attendance on Sundays—along with the general acceptance of prayer as a core religious obligation within the community—meant that there was a great deal of normative pressure for members to visibly respond to the Sunday call to midday prayer when it sounded in the mosque.

Right before the Sunday midday call to prayer, the Muslim Youth Program was usually wrapping up its meeting in the second floor youth room, while parents were generally arriving in the main lobby to pick up their children from Sunday School classes, and older youth were setting up the snack bar in the social hall for their weekly fundraiser. Suddenly, a man's amplified voice would be heard from every corner of the building: "Allaaaaaaaaaa-hu Akbar! Allaaaaaaaaaa-hu Akbar!" A collective pause of quiet hesitation would immediately be followed by a burst of purposeful movement. Men and women would stop their conversations or other activities and start walking toward the prayer hall. Others would move toward the bathroom to perform the obligatory ritual ablution—*wudhu*—before prayer. Religious Director Omar and a few other mosque officials would walk to the front of the prayer hall to prepare to lead the ritual. Inside and around the youth group room upstairs, youth group leaders and other adults would encourage youth to get ready for prayer, saying versions of the following: "Come on, guys, it's time for prayer," "Don't miss prayer, you guys," or "Go, or you'll miss the whole prayer!" As can be seen in this sudden redirection of group attention and movement, communal pressure among the mosque membership strongly encouraged Muslims not only to pray, but to pray *on time*. The urgency with which the adults entreated youth to pray, and with which most adults prepared for the prayer, was testament to the local prioritization of responding to the call to prayer in timely fashion.

In my initial visits to the City Mosque, I too got caught up in this collective post-adhan energy and moved to prepare for prayer as rapidly as possible. After listening to the call, I would briskly walk to the bathroom to perform the ritual ablution if necessary or move directly to the prayer hall. As my fieldwork came to focus more on the Legendz, though, I increasingly found myself in their company at the moment the adhan sounded and started to notice something different: their response—or lack of response—to the Sunday call to midday prayer had a distinct and repeated style. A scene that took place immediately following the adhan one particular Sunday can serve to illustrate the boys' usual response:

> I walk into the youth room and see that Mrs. Habib is there. She tells the boys, "It's time for Dhuhr." [Youth group leader] Shazia asks the group, "Are you guys all going to go down to pray?" None of them really respond to her. Muhammad and Yusef keep chatting. Hazem throws a tennis ball against the back wall of the youth room. Fuad runs after it. I go downstairs and get ready to pray. . . . I go in to pray and stand to the left of Yusef and to the right of an East Asian–looking guy whom I don't know. As I walk out of prayer, I see Muhammad, Abdul, Fuad, and Abshir sitting at the back of the prayer hall; so they did make it to prayers after all.

This scenario was typical. Although the Legendz were literally surrounded by pre-prayer activity and constantly reminded by adults to prepare for prayer, in three and a half years of observation I never saw them once respond to the call to Dhuhr prayer right away. Although they almost always made it to the prayer eventually, they would all initially engage in a visible nonresponse to the call or any adult pleas and then would use the time between the call and the recitation of the prayer—a period of about ten to fifteen minutes—for *anything but* deliberately preparing to pray. They would continue conversations, go to the bathroom, sit down to rest, explore different parts of the mosque and look for their friends, go back outside to briefly play basketball, find something to eat, or play with their smart phones. If they were approached by adults reminding them that it was time to get ready to pray, they would marshal a range of excuses to avoid doing so, including a need to go to the bathroom or "get something," a sense of dizziness, being busy with something else, or needing to wait for someone.

This concentrated burst of activity designed to avoid moving toward the prayer hall before they absolutely *had to* served as a means of tempering what was a powerfully normative and public religious obligation with a brief interlude of autonomous action. In this way, the Legendz used intentional engagement in some activity unrelated to prayer as a means of what Erving Goffman calls "role distancing," that is, interactively portraying a difference between themselves and "the activity the incumbent would engage in were he to act solely in terms of the normative demands of someone in his position."[7] Rather than live out the expected behavior of stereotypically "good Muslim" young men by rushing to prayer, the Legendz exploited the call to prayer as an occasion to subtly differentiate themselves from such a constraining role by intentionally demonstrating the behavioral difference between themselves and those who might respond to the call immediately.

It is not a coincidence that the main example that Goffman uses to illustrate his concept of role distancing is a young person—first aged five years old, then seven or eight, then twelve—riding a merry-go-round. Goffman's hypothetical rider first demonstrates minor "irreverence" toward the wooden horse at the youngest age, then transitions into "bored, nonchalant competence" at the middle age, and, finally, as a preteen, treats "the whole undertaking as a lark, a situation for mockery."[8] Young people often act in ways aimed at differentiating themselves from the adult-approved institutional rules and activities that structure their social surroundings, whether by cutting class and roaming around the hallways at school, making fun of teachers, smoking in and around school, or "resisting" participation in the prom.[9] But when such rules and expectations are not simply part of "adult" institutions like school but are also central to their own identity, community, or family—as in the case of "traditional" expectations of behavior within religious and immigrant contexts—then engagement in nonparticipation is less clear cut. In these cases, immigrant and highly religious youth find creative ways to express evidence of individualistic behavior within courses of action that still generally hew to communal norms: Young Punjabi women in California add jewelry and makeup to their otherwise traditional clothing while on the way to school. Students at an evangelical Christian school use a couple of free moments before class to talk exclusively about "secular" culture—television, music, and dating. Hasidic Jewish girls, swimming at an all-female pool, leave their long robes and stockings off for slightly longer than they are permitted.[10] In these ways, as in the Legendz's approach to prayer, otherwise rule-following youth find ways to demonstrate a small but visible distinction between themselves and the traditional behavior in which they participate.

Young adult staff members of the Muslim Youth Program occasionally lent support to the Legendz's approach to prayer by allowing them to delay prayers if they were busy doing something important, especially when they felt that the youth could be trusted to fulfill the obligation eventually. This was the case with Yusef, whose consistently normative Islamic practice earned him the trust of the young adult leaders. One Friday when the call to evening prayer was sounded during the mosque's Spiritual Night, youth leader Melvin could not find Yusef. Melvin saw Tariq standing near the youth room and asked him, "Where's Yusef?"

Tariq replied, "I think he's downstairs closing up the grill."

Melvin shrugged and said, "Okay, I guess he can pray later." In small ways like this, young leaders demonstrated to youth members that praying later was an acceptable way of balancing ritual obligation and individual autonomy.

This resistance to reciting a prayer exactly on time and to getting ready for prayer as soon as an adult or other authority figure demanded was a consistent and consistently observable aspect of the Legendz's religious behavior. The importance of this lax approach to timely prayer to the boys' group identity was evident in the way that Muhammad and the others consistently disparaged young people who emphasized punctuality in prayer. Such a characterization came up one afternoon as I spoke to Muhammad about his cousin Kamal, who had recently immigrated to the United States and was now living near Coast City:

> "Is he very religious?" I ask. Muhammad nods yes energetically with his eyes open wide. "He's always trying to say prayers on time, and [when] we don't want to do it, he just sits there and looks at us like this [imitates him standing there, looking annoyed]. And then we're like, 'OK, OK,' and he's like, 'Thank you.' That guy is annoying sometimes, seriously."

By pushing Muhammad and the others to pray on time, Kamal was threatening one arena in which the Legendz were able to exercise their autonomy in relation to the ritual obligation of prayer—by exercising control over the decision of *when* exactly to do so.

Of course, delaying prayer can also be a means of evading religious obligations altogether. There certainly were times when the Legendz simply skipped prayers or snuck out of the mosque to the back lot when their parents thought they were praying. But, all in all, their attempts to control the when of their prayers were not aimed at moving *away* from religious practice and toward greater autonomy but rather were reflections of their desire to experience and demonstrate personal autonomy in the *midst* of normative religious practice. The way in which experiences of personal autonomy could intertwine with the fulfillment of external obligations was illustrated in an unusually dramatic fashion one Sunday afternoon when a cluster of youth group members, tired of waiting for the religious director, Omar, to arrive to begin prayer, decided to take matters into their own hands. Immediately preceding this episode, Sana, Muhammad, Fuad, and a few other youth were hanging out by the front desk next to the main prayer room. There were people beginning to gather in the prayer area, but the prayer had not started yet. As they continued to wait for the prayer to start, the youth were approached by a mosque staff member named Ibrahim.

Ibrahim says, "Omar wanted us to wait for him for prayer." Sana says, "We're not supposed to wait for a person for prayer. It's about God." Ibrahim says, "I am just speaking in my official role, telling you what Omar told me. If you have a problem, you can tell him." Ali and Aimen say, "Yeah, why are we waiting?"

Omar comes downstairs and runs past the youth into the prayer area to address the assembled group: "I am sorry for being late," he says on the microphone. "We were having a board meeting upstairs about a very important and controversial issue—when to start Ramadan this year." He says this jokingly, but I can't tell if people are laughing or not. . . . Meanwhile, by the front desk, the boys all start walking upstairs. I follow them, assuming they are going to skip prayer and hang out upstairs. But actually, it turns out they are going to pray upstairs in the youth room. "We can't wait forever for Omar," Aimen says to me as we enter the youth room, as if I had asked for an explanation. "It takes too long." "OK, who wants to lead?" Muhammad asks. Ali volunteers. About five of us line up behind him, and he leads us through the prayer. We go through it, and then shake each other's hands and say, "*A salaamu alaikum.*" Fuad says, "They still haven't started."

We all walk downstairs and hang out next to the table set up outside the bookstore. Muhammad excitedly tells Sana and Nailah that we prayed upstairs: "I felt like such a rebel!"

The excitement expressed by Muhammad over participating in a youth-only prayer held at a different time than that of the official mosque prayer demonstrates the sense of autonomy a young person can experience by controlling the particular when and (in this case) where of his or her prayer. Enacting a conventional religious ritual in a slightly different manner allowed Muhammad and the others to experience and display their autonomous religious selves in action, even as they were fulfilling what was still technically a normative religious obligation. This was why Muhammad felt "like such a rebel" after reciting his required daily prayer: he was experiencing the sense of autonomy that comes from introducing a clear alteration to a routine and ritual practice. At the very same time, though, even this change took place within the framework of Muhammed's required and expected religious duty—praying his afternoon daily prayer. In this way, the Legendz still strove to meet their ritual obligations, but in a slightly and visibly different fashion than they believed a stereotypical "good Muslim" would.

Invoking the "Extreme Muslim" to Project Reflexivity and Protect Autonomy

Another mechanism that allowed the Legendz to generate a sense of youthful American individuality amid communal religious participation was the strategic invocation of the "extreme Muslim" during interactions. Regularly referenced by the Legendz and other mosque youth, the extreme Muslim was an embodied and voiced caricature who stood as a crude representation of an unreflexive and harshly imposed Islam against which the City Mosque youth could position themselves in contrast as reflexive, freethinking, and tolerant young Muslims.

One instance of such an invocation took place during a youth group meeting one Sunday afternoon. During this session, a guest teacher led an exercise in which the youth group members acted out skits about challenging issues that they faced in their day-to-day lives. In one such skit, focused on the topic of "gossip," Ali and Lena (who always wore a hijab) played two young people sitting next to each other at a coffee shop while checking Facebook on a computer and talking about their friends. Upon entering the scene, youth program member Adam took the opportunity to imitate and invoke the extreme Muslim, even though the figure was not particularly relevant to the topic:

Ali and Lena sit next to each other, pretending to look at a computer and gossip about their friends. Adam walks in, as one of the café workers, and says to Lena, in a loud, harsh voice and with an exaggerated "Arab" accent: "You are wearing a headscarf? You are supposed to be Muslims!" The audience laughs. He then turns to both of them sitting together and, in the same voice, says, "There must be 16 inches between a man and a woman!" He chops his hand between their two seats to make his point. Saif, playing the other café worker, adopts the same voice and asks, "Is zis ze real Muslim?" Kids in the audience roar with laughter.

As can be seen here, the extreme Muslim was generally invoked through an imitation in which mosque youth would adopt an exaggerated vocal style, heavy accent, and loud volume, signifying a stereotypically older, male, first-generation immigrant Muslim. The extreme Muslim's tone of voice was always harsh and commanding, and every time he appeared, he imposed strict religious rules aggressively and oppressively on others. This, then, was the stylistic *form* of the extreme Muslim imitation. Many youth at the mosque, whether male or female, younger or older, or of various ethnic backgrounds, could easily mimic the widely recognized voice and mannerisms of the extreme Muslim during everyday interaction. As with all imitations, the extreme Muslim caricature served to demonstrate that those who performed the role as well as those who got the joke were in fact *different from* the imitated figure. Like American high school boys who regularly imitate "fags" to assure one another of their own heterosexuality, the Legendz's ability to step into and then out of the extreme Muslim character was proof that they were not themselves extreme Muslims.[11] Regular imitation of the extreme Muslim was a way for the Legendz and other mosque youth to repeatedly invoke the "threatening specter"[12] of an undesirable identity—the unthinking, judgmental, and overly strict religious Muslim—from whom these youth could repeatedly differentiate themselves.

The extreme Muslim could pop up almost anywhere—during an official youth group meeting, in casual conversation behind the mosque, on a trip to 7-Eleven, in someone's car. The *content* of these imitations—that is, the words uttered in the voice of the extreme Muslim—revolved around a strict and harsh regulation of behaviors that were actually considered generally *permissible* within the City Mosque community. In other words, invoking the extreme Muslim served as a reminder that while other kinds of Muslims might have a problem with a certain behavior, the City Mosque community, and especially its youth members, did not. Accordingly, the themes most often brought up in extreme Muslim imitations reflected the two dimensions of behavior through which City Mosque members tended to distinguish themselves from other, more "conservative," Muslims, namely, participation in American youth culture and gender relations. In both cases, the implicit critique communicated through these imitations was that the extreme Muslim was not sophisticated enough to make distinctions between different kinds of youth- or gender-related behaviors so as to determine which of them were actually Islamically inappropriate and therefore worth getting worked up about. Instead, the extreme Muslim crudely labeled every kind of American youth culture behavior as haram and lumped nearly all forms of association between unmarried men and women together in viewing them as religiously forbidden.

One afternoon, Yusef invoked the youth culture–related variant of the extreme Muslim in the mosque parking lot shortly after the Legendz performed a series of hip hop songs as part of a mosque-sponsored youth arts showcase.

> The Legendz walk off the front of the stage and energetically give dap to their friends who arrived while they were sound checking—Sayed, Ali, and some older-looking guys who I don't know. They stand in a cluster and talk. Ali is wearing a black collared shirt and nice-looking slacks. Muhammad says to him, "Why are you dressed up?" Ali says, "I'm going to a party later." Yusef says, in his harsh-toned Arab accent, "You dress up for a party, but not for zee mosque? Parties are haram!" Ali shakes his head and laughs.

In this case, the extreme Muslim was portrayed as obsessed with religious propriety and thus unable to demonstrate a more reflexive or nuanced approach to the negotiation of religious rules. The mere mention of a party set this "specter" off on an aggressive attack against *all* parties. The implication here was that "we"—the youth who performed hip hop and were practicing Muslims—did not share this unthinking and overly strict perspective on youth culture and were able to both engage in youth culture and maintain Islamic identity and practice. Outbursts in the voice of the extreme Muslim throughout the day—in response to a friend's audible ring tone in the mosque ("Music? In zee *masjid* [mosque]?"), dancing ("Danzing iz haram!"), or an R-rated movie at someone's home ("What is *zis*?")—allowed the Legendz to interactionally formulate a "constitutive outside"[13] containing crude and harsh perspectives on youth cultural practices. In opposition to this specter of judgmental and unreflexive Islam, the Legendz promoted themselves as reflexive and freethinking Muslims who both allowed such practices to continue and still believed that they were good Muslims.

The concern most frequently voiced by the extreme Muslim caricature focused on rules regulating gender interaction and women's behavior. At the City Mosque, where young men and women were permitted to sit next to each other in the youth program and women held visible and important leadership positions, the repeated invocation of a specter with a more gender-restrictive Islamic perspective served to reinforce a sense of shared commitment to a more moderate approach to gender issues. Youth imitated the extreme Muslim in order to caricature locally undesirable gender practices, including the strict segregation of males and females ("Do not crozz *zis* line!"), the enforcement of a female dress code ("Pleez cover your arms!"), and the insistence that women not make direct eye contact with men so as to uphold their modesty ("Lower your gaze, sisters!"). This thematic thread in the extreme Muslim's outbursts revealed a concerted effort among young mosque members to differentiate themselves symbolically from those Muslims whom they considered to be overly obsessed with regulating women's behavior and dress.

One Friday evening, while hanging out with Abdul and Tariq near the basketball court behind the mosque, I had an unexpected encounter with this gender-obsessed version of the extreme Muslim. I suddenly remembered that Muhammad had told me that he would be working at the front desk that night, so I decided to walk inside and say hello.

After telling Abdul and Tariq what I'm doing, I head inside. As I walk through the social hall, I hear a voice echoing over the mosque's sound system, giving a lecture about the Qur'an. I notice that the voice is quite high and so I assume that it is a woman giving the talk. As I walk past the prayer area towards Muhammad at the front desk, though, I turn to my right and see that it is in fact a man giving the lecture. When I reach Muhammad at the front desk, I tell him, "I thought that was a woman speaking." Muhammad puts on a heavy "Arab" accent and an expression of mock horror, and says, "Astaghfirullah [God forgive you], bruzzer! A woman addressing the masjid [mosque]? Zis is not right! What do you want to have next? A stripper in ze mosque? Would you want to put a stripper over zere instead of the bookstore? [he points to the bookstore]. Maybe you think zis would be a good way to raise money, because no one is buying ze books? Maybe you are right." I laugh through this whole speech.

Enactment of the gender- and youth culture–obsessed extreme Muslim helped cultivate a sense of solidarity among youth at the mosque in two ways. First, the *form* of the imitation—loud voice, heavy accent, and aggressive tone—signified an important difference between those participating in the present interaction and those more extreme Muslims "out there" along the dimension of *style*. One of the messages sent by these imitations was that this forceful, harsh, and loud manner was not "our" way of speaking about Islamic rules. Second, the specific *content* of the imitations—the gender- and youth-related regulations that mosque members widely agreed were unnecessary to being a good Muslim—served to differentiate participants from those "other Muslims" along the dimension of *substantive* Islamic concerns. A second message sent through such imitations was that these particular regulations on youth and female life, such as denying women visible roles in the mosque, declaring various kinds of music impermissible, policing women's dress, and disallowing all youth "parties," were not approaches to Islamic life that "we" supported.

By repeatedly distancing themselves from specific modes of Islamic religious life through this symbolic means, the Legendz and their friends also enacted a specific expectation of young, modern American cultural subjects, namely, the demonstration of a distanced "reflexivity" toward their own religious identities. It is generally accepted among sociologists that reflexivity—the ability to "step back" and critically reflect on one's own culture and tradition—is an expectation of modern, individual subjects, and particularly young people.[14] For the Legendz and their friends, not only did the extreme Muslim offer a way to differentiate themselves from more conservative Muslims, but the interactive act of this differentiation itself—an ironic imitation of a crude and essentialized version of Islam—served as an immediate and embodied demonstration of their general ability to step back and be momentarily "outside" of their religious and cultural identity. In this way, the imitation of the extreme Muslim allowed the Legendz to demonstrate a culturally American and modern young self through repeated, embodied reflexive behavior.

Other young people growing up in situations of cultural contestation between "traditional" religious or immigrant communities and the broader American culture as experienced through public school and the media have also been found to use symbolic specters of "overly" religious or ethnic figures to cast themselves as more acceptably reflexive, moderate, and American. Young Hasidic women working to position themselves as modern people talk disparagingly of "nebs"—young women who are too stringently religious, unfashionable, and fluent in Yiddish.[15] Students at an evangelical Christian high school angling for a moderate religious identity continually refer to stereotypes of extremely religious young people whom they try *not* to be like: "Mr. Righteous," "Miss Pious," "Joe Bible," and "Miss God."[16] Similarly, second-generation Iranian youth at a heritage summer camp perform heavily accented versions of their parents and other community members in a way that signifies affection but also makes the youth seem less culturally bound and more American than the older generation.[17] It is important to note that neither these behaviors nor the use of the extreme Muslim by the Legendz necessarily signified a rejection of communal life, the older generation, or cultural tradition in general. Rather, they were ways for young people growing up in such a community to assure themselves and each other of their autonomy and reflexivity, even as they existed in a communal cultural context.

The "Extreme Muslim" and Interpersonal Religious Accountability

When directed at issues on which it could be safely assumed all community members agreed, imitation of the extreme Muslim was an effective means of cultivating a sense of group cohesion and warmth, often expressed through shared laughter. Centered on a common religious approach and shared communicative style, the caricature allowed members a chance to present themselves as modern, reflexive subjects. The practice of mimicking the extreme Muslim in order to cultivate solidarity was usually linked to perspectives on Islamic behavior that all in-group members were assumed to share. Occasionally, however, the extreme Muslim discourse played a different, more specific role in the daily lives of the Legendz, that is, as a socially acceptable means through which to comment on the potentially un-Islamic behavior of another young Muslim.

According to the City Mosque's teachings, one important part of being a Muslim was encouraging co-religionists to uphold Islamically appropriate behavior, or, in the words of the youth program's slogan, to "help Muslims to become better Muslims." The expectations of individual autonomy associated with American youth culture, however, are at odds with the practice of directly telling another young person how to act or what to do. Indeed, in the Legendz's community, a young person who tried to tell another young person what to do in terms of religious practices or behaviors was quickly and consistently branded as "annoying," someone they "didn't like," or, referencing the mosque's religious director, a "little Omar." To manage the particular dilemma of being expected to hold fellow Muslims to account but at the same time wishing not to be seen as infringing on the personal autonomy of a peer, the Legendz and their friends strategically resorted to the voice of the extreme Muslim at these potentially troublesome moments.

One of the first times I noticed such a use of the extreme Muslim voice was on a late Sunday afternoon during my first summer at the mosque. The youth group had let out hours earlier, and Melvin and I were sitting in the quiet lobby of the mosque talking to a young man named Zaid who had recently joined the group. The conversation consisted mostly of Melvin, an African American young adult staff member of the youth program, complaining about how challenging it was to meet potential marriage partners in the local Muslim community, since many parents strongly preferred their children to marry people from within their ethnic or national group. As the conversation became more intimate and the comfortable rhythm of the talking suggested growing ease and familiarity, Melvin suggested, "Why don't we go upstairs?"

> The three of us climb the stairs up from the downstairs lobby to just outside of the youth group room. Melvin leads us into the empty youth group room. Zaid sits on top of one of the stacks of chairs against the wall, and Melvin and I sit at chairs at a small folding table. Zaid asks Melvin, "Do you care who you marry by race?" "No," Melvin says. "I mean," says Zaid, "do you have a preference?" Melvin says, "I don't have one." Zaid says, "How about an interest in a certain culture?" Melvin says, "To me, it's all about the person." He then looks over his shoulder, lowers his voice, and leans towards us: "I know I'm not supposed to say this, but I've dated other people." Zaid puts on an Arab accent and says, "You will go to zee masjid and you will ask for forgiveness!" Melvin, seemingly unfazed, says, "I went to Mecca and asked for forgiveness. That should last me for a while."

In contrast to the more general deployment of the extreme Muslim discussed previously, here the behavior in question—dating before marriage—was something that was clearly considered (at least in public) un-Islamic within the local City Mosque context. Consequently, Melvin's revelation of a behavior that he himself suggested was problematic put Zaid in a tough position, one fraught with potential conflict. If Zaid criticized Melvin's admittedly un-Islamic behavior too directly, he risked being seen as too strict or as a "little

Omar" by Melvin, who might have taken this judgment as a threat to his own sense of autonomy and independence. If Zaid did not comment on this behavior, he would not have been acting in a manner consistent with the expectations of his religious community and his own sense of Muslim identity. In order to manage this dilemma, Zaid did what the Legendz and their friends almost always did in situations like this: he invoked the specter of the extreme Muslim *at the very moment* of commenting on another young person's potentially un-Islamic behavior. In fact, the commentary and mimicry occurred simultaneously, since Zaid used the voice of the extreme Muslim to suggest that Melvin needed to ask for forgiveness for his past actions.

This directed use of the extreme Muslim helped minimize the potential trouble that the interaction with Melvin could have initiated by injecting a reminder of the boys' shared culture at the precise moment that the friend's behavior was being criticized. First, the reference to a popular joke among mosque youth—one meant to poke fun at adults—served to remind Melvin that he and Zaid both saw themselves as clever, funny, and self-reflexive young Muslims in opposition to others who were "too religiously serious" and that they also shared a common history with such jokes. Second, by invoking the aggressive interpersonal style of the extreme Muslim, Zaid drew attention to a *style* of interpersonal religious accountability that both agreed was highly undesirable but also that he was mimicking and therefore *not actually using* in this interaction. Thus, pretending to be the extreme Muslim while reminding another youth of a religious rule was essentially a way of saying, "Even though I am doing this, I am not like them." The ironic and exaggerated evocation of the extreme Muslim *style* neutralized the threat that Melvin might have felt from this admonition had it been issued without this symbolic gesture. As a result, he was comfortable accepting and earnestly responding to the *content* of Zaid's comment—the suggestion that he ask for forgiveness.

During my time with the Legendz, I regularly witnessed the use of the extreme Muslim persona to comment on the potentially un-Islamic behavior of other youth in a way that would not be perceived as threatening to their sense of autonomous personhood. This strategy was effectively exploited to alter a range of specific behaviors that were locally considered Islamically inappropriate, such as listening to music, cursing, or dancing in the mosque; lying next to a member of the opposite sex on a beach; or talking about recreational drug use. In nearly every case, the use of this strategy led the recipient of such comments to modify his or her behavior without expressing frustration at being told to do so. Use of the extreme Muslim was even directed at me one day when I accompanied Tariq, Muhammad, Salman, and Fuad to 7-Eleven to get some snacks.

As we browse the shelves, the boys stop by the racks of magazines by the front door and begin flipping through different ones. Muhammad leafs though the pages of a hip hop magazine. Fuad and Tariq look at car magazines. Salman reads a skating magazine. I notice a picture of the actress Jenna Fischer from the show *The Office* on the cover of a health magazine and I pull it out of the rack. She's wearing a small bikini on the cover. Tariq sees me pull this up and says, "Astaghfirullah! [God forgive you!] John O'Brien is looking at naked women! Zis is haram!" I drop the magazine into the rack, feeling slightly embarrassed. I say, "That's not why I was looking at that." "John O'Brien!" Muhammad says, with mock horror.

While I certainly felt embarrassed by Fuad's pointing at the magazine I was looking at, I did not feel upset. The invocation of the extreme Muslim and Muhammad's joking comment served to cushion this act of interpersonal Islamic correction with familiar humor, irony, and reflexivity. More importantly, I *did* drop the magazine and therefore alter my behavior to become more Islamically appropriate. The directed use of the extreme Muslim was thus a means of encouraging Muslim peers to change their behavior, but in a way that sought to protect their sense of autonomy and independence.

Emphasizing Individual Effort in the Realization of Religious Behavior

If one way of constructing a more individualistic Islamic self involved making slight alterations to prayer in order to demonstrate a degree of autonomy from communal influence, and another consisted of emphasizing one's own reflexivity and autonomy in contrast to an unreflective and overly authoritative form of Islam, a third centered on speaking in ways that stressed one's individual agency, or personal effort, in realizing Islamically appropriate behavior. In using terms and tones aimed at emphasizing the central role of an effortful, agentive self in the achievement of rightly religious action, the Legendz downplayed the influence of external religious and communal authority. While the central meanings expressed through the acts of altering prayer time and invoking the extreme Muslim were those of autonomy (freedom from social influence) and reflexivity (a "stepping back" that allowed one to consider one's tradition and culture), the main meaning expressed by the act of framing religious behavior as the result of individual effort was that of *agency*. Although at first glance the difference between agency and autonomy may seem slight and difficult to distinguish, the distinction is an important one to recognize when it comes to understanding the multifaceted ways in which the Legendz worked to construct a religious practice more in tune with American culture.

"Agency" continues to be one of the most contested and vexing terms in sociology.[18] For the purposes of this chapter, however, I use a conservative definition of the term to refer to visible "individual effort." This sense of the word, and its clear differentiation from autonomy, is rooted in the work of anthropologist Saba Mahmood. In her ethnography of the female mosque movement in Egypt, Mahmood critiques the tendency of feminist and other "liberal" scholars to equate agency with movement *against* tradition or norms. Instead, she argues, agency must be de-linked from "political and moral autonomy" so that social agents, such as her intentionally pious and self-restricting subjects, can be seen as agentive even in their embrace and fulfillment of social constraints.[19] Separating agency from autonomy in this way is useful for my analysis as well, because the Legendz sometimes took individual action and, more significantly, emphasized their own active efforts while engaged in practices that were in large part imposed by tradition and community.

When it came to discussing their own Islamic actions, the boys repeatedly used the self-celebrating tones of urban braggadocio to highlight the individual effort they put into bringing about their own ethical behavior. I witnessed this kind of rhetorical ownership over right religious action one evening as I accompanied the Legendz to a concert and dance at a private high school that was attended by a few of their female friends from the mosque. The event involved bands playing hip hop and ska music, as well as boys and girls dancing together, though not in very intimate ways. When the dance wound down at around 9 p.m., the school principal and other adults encouraged all the students to go home and not linger. As we headed out of the auditorium, the boys walked intermingled with a cluster of girls, some from the mosque, others whom they had just met, through the darkening parking lot toward Muhammad's car.

> Our little group stops by one car, and Aisha says goodbye to everyone. Sara says goodbye to us all as well. Aisha hugs everyone, and then Sara does, too. I stand near Yusef and Sara as they hug, and then I hear her say something about "weird" to Yusef. The rest of the group—the boys, the girl who hosted the dance, and Aisha's other friend—keep walking further into the parking lot. I ask Yusef, "What did Sara say?" He says, "She said it feels weird to hug like that." "Oh," I say, nodding. Then he says, "But I don't trip because it's OK if your mind is in the right place. And *my* mind was in the right place." I nod. We keep walking towards the car.

Yusef's delivery of the phrase "*My* mind was in the right place," with marked emphasis on the word "my" and the cadence of an urban boast, communicated that this religiously appropriate act was *his* doing, and that *he* therefore deserved credit for it. He and I both knew, however, that he was following a communally derived regulation regarding male–female interaction. Only a week earlier, Omar had spoken to the youth group about exchanging hugs with females in public, saying that because it was a common custom in the United States, it *was* acceptable to do so, but only as long as one's intentions were religiously pure. Given this context, Yusef made sure to attribute the proper fulfillment of this obligation to his *own* actions, thereby obscuring the role of communal pressure or guidance and framing Islamically right behavior as his own individual achievement.

This desire to frame Islamic action as the result of individual effort rather than simply a response to community expectations or parental or adult pressure was also manifested one Sunday afternoon at the mosque when a few of the boys began recounting an incident that had taken place at a conference of a statewide Muslim organization that they had attended with some young women from the mosque the previous week. As Muhammad and Abdul told the story of how Muhammad had been approached by one of the conference staff members, Carlos (a non-Muslim friend of the boys) and I listened:

> Muhammad says, "This guy came over and told us we were sitting too close to the sisters [young women], just because Sana and I were sitting just like this." He indicates how he and Abdul are currently sitting—next to each other, about three inches apart. Muhammad and Abdul both look incredulous about this. "And Sana is," Abdul says, "well, she is like our sister. . . . I mean, if you have a problem seeing every girl you see in that way, then that's on you, but *I'm* not like that."

The Legendz consistently referred to their religious behaviors in ways that presented their fulfillment of Islamic obligations as evidence of their individual skill and effort rather than as simply the dutiful following of an overarching culture or tradition or a mindless bowing to pressure from parents or other adults. Their individualizing language and tone always took the form of urban bragging and tended to crop up in situations in which there was a clear religiously and communally derived expectation of what action should be taken. During a youth group discussion on whether it was possible to both do the Islamically right thing and gain the respect of non-Muslim peers, Yusef, whose working-class urban neighborhood was rife with gang activity and delinquency, observed, "For me, I'm myself. I always get pressure: 'Come drink a 40,' 'We'll smoke you out.' But I stay true to myself." Here again, Yusef was emphasizing his central role in decision-making by describing his choice as staying true to *himself* rather than to Islam or religious leaders while at the same time adhering to what was commonly known to be a communally enforced religious norm—abstention from alcohol and other intoxicating substances. Other members of the group similarly emphasized their agency by actively pointing to their participation in normative behaviors in situations such as considering girls in a sexual way (*"I'm* not like that!"), taking soda to a teenage party where alcohol was served ("We brought our *own* drinks, homey!"), or dispensing advice on the best way to fast on a hot day ("You just have to know how to *do* it"). In each case, the boys' assertion of active engagement in Islamically normative behavior while emphasizing personal effort rather than obedience to a divine or adult authority helped demonstrate and differentiate an agentive self, even in the course of fulfilling a religious obligation.

Portraying a self who exercises control over his or her behavior instead of bowing to external constraints is a core expectation of American culture.[20] When this expectation meets a cultural context in which communal and religious authority is considered paramount, young people caught in the middle find creative ways of responding. Evangelical Christian high school students "profess independence" and talk about themselves in ways that emphasize their own active role in their religious lives even if they rarely deviate from the norm.[21] Young Latina Catholics reassure one another that being a virgin is "cool," even if this stance clashes with their peer culture, because it is something they do themselves—as a "choice"—rather than because of parental or community pressure.[22] And evangelical Christian college students discuss their decisions not to drink or engage in premarital sex using language that "portray[s] themselves as more mature or more controlled" than their non-Christian peers.[23] In each of these cases, as with the Legendz, young people who experience a culturally contested social position work to make that position more tenable through the application of discourses of individualism amid communal culture.

Conclusion

This chapter has detailed the everyday practices used by the Legendz and their friends to manage a specific cultural dilemma faced by Muslim American youth: how to participate in a religious tradition that carries expectations of deference to external religious authority and obligation within a modern American cultural landscape in which personal agency, autonomy, and reflexivity are core social values and widely held behavioral expectations. The Legendz responded to this challenge by engaging in practices associated with one particular cultural rubric (religious Islam) while applying discourses and behavior associated with the other (American individualism). In this way, they attempted to present themselves as agentive, autonomous, and self-reflexive American youth despite their regular fulfillment of externally imposed Islamic obligations. In altering the specifics of prayer through visible temporal delays, the boys attempted to demonstrate an autonomous yet Islamic self to themselves and each other. By invoking the specter of the "extreme Muslim" in conversation, they presented themselves as self-reflexive Islamic individuals—ones not unthinkingly beholden to strict religious requirements—while protecting the autonomy of their peers by displacing religious authority in interaction. In applying the speech patterns of urban braggadocio when recounting their participation in Muslim moral behavior, they attempted to infuse communally rooted norms with a sense of individual agency. Through these ongoing, patterned everyday practices, the Legendz strove to recast normative religious actions as compatible with, rather than opposed to, notions of American individualism.

While these practices of symbolic individualism certainly did not lead to "real" or complete freedom from influence or social independence for the Legendz, they did make a consequential and significant difference in how the boys experienced their religious and communal lives. Discursive forms of individualism allowed the Legendz to experience a subjective sense of autonomy and agency, at least at specific moments, even if these experiences were in fact hemmed in by objective communal constraints. When Muhammad claimed that he felt "like a rebel" after leading an all-youth prayer, when Yusef insisted that *his* mind was in the right place when he hugged a female, and when all the boys interactively set themselves in opposition to the "extreme Muslim," they were experiencing themselves as agentive, autonomous, and self-reflexive American subjects despite the fact that their actions were also heavily influenced by communal Islamic expectations. Their subjectively experienced sense of individualism was important not only for the momentary respite that it granted them in their lives of communal obligation, but also because when enough of these experiences were strung together in patterned and institutionally permitted ways, an Islamic lifestyle began to feel compatible with an American cultural context.

This chapter also suggests that the Legendz and their generational peers were developing a local, Islamic version of what sociologists of religion in America have called "religious individualism." According to the classic formulation, religious individualism is a way of practicing religion in America, primarily among members of the Christian majority, that emphasizes the privatization of spiritual practice over communal religious participation and widely sees religious commitment as a voluntary choice rather than an inherited obligation. In his highly influential book *Habits of the Heart*, Robert Bellah expresses concern that the increasing presence of individualistic language and culture within American religious traditions is drawing Americans away from communal, religious lives.[24] In addition to demonstrating a youthful, Islamic version of religious individualism at work, this chapter suggests that the infusion of meanings associated with broader individualistic culture into tightly knit religious communities need not weaken communal participation or commitment. On the contrary, the case of the Legendz demonstrates how an ongoing ability to signify allegiance with American expectations of individualism in the course of communal commitment can help modern religious actors *maintain* legitimate membership in their local cultural communities. As ongoing and subjectively meaningful mechanisms for expressing and experiencing a sense of culturally American selfhood, the Legendz's practices of discursive individualism worked to make their communally and social circumscribed Islamic commitments more congruent with their American cultural context and more palatable and even enjoyable to their youthful American selves.

4

"Keeping It Halal" and Dating While Muslim

TWO KINDS OF MUSLIM ROMANTIC RELATIONSHIPS

The Problem of Dating

It's a Sunday afternoon in November, and I'm sitting in the packed community room of the City Mosque flanked by Muhammad and Zaki on my left and two young women from the youth group, May and Noor, on my right. The 150-person-capacity hall is filled with chattering adults and young people, but Omar has asked that the first few rows be reserved for youth group members because today's speaker "wants to speak directly to the youth." As usual, the modest stage at the front of the room is adorned with an American flag on one side and a flag representing the City Mosque on the other. Gold letters spelling out "City Mosque" span the back wall, and large photographs of significant holy sites—the Dome of the Rock in Jerusalem and the Masjid Al Haram in Mecca—hang on the wall at either end of the stage. The crowd quiets down as a middle-aged woman dressed in a white-collared shirt, black pants, and no headscarf approaches the podium to introduce the main speaker: "Dr. Lang is a math professor at the University of Kansas and has become a well-known author and speaker on Islam since he converted over twenty years ago. Please welcome Dr. Jeffrey Lang." The crowd bursts into enthusiastic applause.

I first heard about Jeffrey Lang in the early 2000s, when I was approaching my own conversion to Islam. He was an author recommended to me by many acquaintances—both converts and born Muslims—as someone who had written thoughtfully about the opportunities and challenges of becoming a Muslim in America. Until today, however, I had not realized how highly esteemed he was among many immigrant and American-born Muslims as a thoughtful commentator on some of the most challenging issues facing Muslims in the United States.

As Lang speaks about issues ranging from gender inequality in mosques and ethnic division in the Muslim community to the challenge of young people leaving the religion, the audience in the community hall listens with rapt attention. But the issue that seems to strike the gathered crowd with the greatest impact this afternoon—judging at least from the considerable murmurs, seat shifting, and nervous laughter that occur during this stretch of his talk—is the topic of courtship and marriage among young Muslims.

Near the end of his speech, Lang informs his listeners, "One man e-mailed me and said, 'My twelve-year-old daughter asked me, "Daddy, how am I going to get married?"'" Murmurs pass through the crowd. "And the father said, 'We'll set you up with someone from back home.' And then the daughter said, 'Really, Daddy, how am I going to get married?'" Widespread laughter consumes the crowd, as if they are releasing a collective tension. Lang continues, "This is a real problem in our communities. If young people are not meeting each other and getting married, this is a real problem. Right now, many of our young Muslims are marrying non-Muslims. Also, many of them are marrying women from their parents' home countries, which means you have many Muslim young women in this country with few prospects for finding Muslim men to marry." There is more murmuring among the crowd. "One young woman put it this way: 'My father says I can't talk to Muslim boys, so I don't know any

Muslim boys. So at school, the only boys I talk to are non-Muslims, so I know a lot of non-Muslim boys.'" People in the crowd laugh with what seems like recognition. "This is the situation we face."

———

While on this occasion, the presence of an outside speaker provided an opportunity for open and honest talk about premarital gender relationships in Muslim American communities, the vexing and contradictory nature of courtship practices among observant young Muslims was not news to any of the young people at the City Mosque. On the contrary, most of the boys in the Legendz had been involved in different kinds of dating relationships since their middle school years. While the dating challenges these young men faced were not the same as those faced by young women in the City Mosque community, who encountered far greater restrictions in navigating courtship, they still had to wrestle with the contradiction of being drawn to the teenage rituals of romantic love while being consistently exposed to and inculcated with communal expectations of abstinence and restraint in their relations with the opposite sex.

As with many other young people growing up in religiously conservative or second-generation immigrant families or communities, the Legendz's desire to date placed them in a situation of cultural tension between the social expectations for appropriate courtship as defined by their parents, community leaders, and other adults and the norms of American teenage romantic life as demonstrated by school peers, mainstream media, and popular culture.[1] According to the American model of heterosexual youth courtship, young men and women were to make their own decisions to become romantically involved and pursue such relationships independent of their families, often in private, and with the expectation of experiencing increasing levels of physical intimacy, potentially up to sexual intercourse. In the City Mosque model of premarital gender relationships, young men and women were to pursue courtship only with the full knowledge of their parents, with the overt intention of marriage, with no physical intimacy or sex, and with no time spent alone together. One day Omar explained this last restriction to the youth group with a colorful example, stating that when two young people of different genders are alone together, temptation may follow because "the third person in the room is *Shaitan* [Satan]." For young practicing Muslim American teenagers who want to date, as the Legendz did, the question was *how* to participate in both of these socially intersecting cultural rubrics with a minimum of conflict and social stress.

By the fall of 2009, about two and a half years into my time with the Legendz, the boys were older and entering new phases of adolescence. Fuad and Tariq were now seventeen, Abdul was eighteen and beginning his senior year of high school, and Yusef and Muhammad, the older brothers in the crew, were both nineteen. Salman, the group's "kid cousin," was thirteen and, as usual, trying to act like and hang out with the older Legendz as much as possible. From fall to spring of 2009, all of the boys became more visibly interested and involved in romantic relationships at around the same time, despite their different ages. During this same period, they also became increasingly open to talking about these relationships with each other and with me.

As their interest in and engagement with dating became more noticeable, two indigenous social solutions to the dilemma of participating in romantic relationships as young religious Muslims became apparent. The first, exemplified by Yusef and Salman, centered on seeking and emphasizing compatibility between the cultural rubrics of Islamically appropriate courtship behavior and American-style teenage dating. Labeling their dating relationships halal (Islamically appropriate), setting explicit limits on physical intimacy, and emphasizing emotional similarities between romantic and religious devotion allowed these young men to consider these two templates for cultural action as potentially in sync. Adopting the boys' own term, I call this compatibility-oriented model of dating "keeping it halal." While this approach to dating seemed quite attractive to Yusef and Salman at first, the model's explicit Islamic framing—initially seen as advantageous—set up idealized expectations for behavior that were quite difficult to maintain over time and were significantly at odds with the cultural expectations of mainstream American teenage romance that surrounded them. Eventually, these boys found it too frustrating to keep it halal and stopped using this model for dating altogether.

In the second model of dating, exemplified by Abdul, Muhammad, and Fuad, the young men actively resisted attempts to set their romantic relationships within an Islamic cultural framework, avoided speaking about physical intimacy with any specificity, and incorporated community-associated courtship practices into their dating in low-key, rather than explicit, ways. I term this second model of young Muslim dating, which was grounded in sustained practices of interactional ambiguity and understatement rather than specificity and clarity, "dating while Muslim." Dating while Muslim seemed to lead to romantic teenage relationships among Muslim youth that were less stressful and more sustainable than those based on the "keeping it halal" model.

Dating at the Mosque

The first time I heard anything about the Legendz's involvement in romantic relationships was in the fall of 2008, during my second year at the City Mosque. One weekend day, a group of about twenty youth and a few adults from the mosque took an organized trip to a local amusement park. Fuad and Abshir rode in my car, while the other kids, including Abdul, took a large van. As we drove down the highway, Fuad and Abshir kept making joking references to Abdul's "girlfriend," so I asked them about it directly:

"So does Abdul really have a girlfriend?" Fuad says, "Yeah." Abshir says, "It's that girl Yasmin, she's Mr. Hanafi's daughter." "Oh," I say. Muhammad says, "If Mr. Hanafi knew, he would kick Abdul's ass." They both laugh. "That's why I thought it was kind of crazy that he put it on his Facebook," I say. "But he didn't say who it was," Abshir says quickly. "So, who knows about it?" I ask them. "Just the family," Fuad says, meaning the Legendz, I think. "Ooooooh," he continues, "imagine if Mr. Hanafi caught Abdul trying to do something. Damn." Abshir says, "When Abdul's older, he's gonna need to talk to Mr. Hanafi to get his permission to get married. Yeah, maybe they'll get married. It's like an arranged marriage or something." Fuad says, "No, I don't think they're gonna get married." Abshir says, "Abdul's mom would kick his butt, too, if she knew about it." "I know," Fuad says.

Later, at the amusement park, Abdul, who was then fifteen, confirmed this for me, telling me that Yasmin was his "girlfriend" but nothing else—most likely because his mother was nearby. Now that I knew about this relationship, I tried to watch how Abdul and Yasmin interacted when they were in the same place, but they rarely seemed to even speak to one another. The next time I heard about their relationship was a year later, when Abdul told me that Yasmin had "left him for a Mexican" a few months earlier.

The relationships that the Legendz took part in up until late 2009 were all similar to the one that I observed between Abdul and Yasmin. These arrangements were with girls whom they knew from either the mosque or school, were hidden from parents and mosque leaders, and were generally of a short-term or on-and-off nature. Beginning in the fall of 2009, however, the boys all began participating in more serious relationships at around the same time. These later relationships were exclusively with young Muslim women and took up more time and focus than their earlier "girlfriend" arrangements had. I watched as attention previously devoted to peer group activities such as skateboarding, basketball, and joking around was redirected to managing and negotiating activities involving girlfriends: spending hours on the phone and texting, arranging ways to spend time alone together, giving and receiving tokens of affection such as flowers and cookies, sneaking opportunities to get close to each other in and around the mosque, flirting at community events, and writing romantic songs and poems. In short, dating and romantic relationships became much more central to the Legendz's lives.

Growing attention to romance and attraction is, of course, not unusual for adolescents. In this case, however, the emerging priorities of romantic love and commitment needed to be managed in relation to a preexisting set of social expectations already central to the lives of the Legendz, namely, Islamic practice and halal behavior. As it turned out, each of the Legendz attempted to participate in some form of romantic dating while simultaneously maintaining some legitimate level of involvement with Islam and their Muslim community. This chapter's exploration of two distinct models for dating as a Muslim American teenager reveals important variations in the practical management of Muslim subjectivity as it comes into contact with competing templates of cultural action. More generally, it suggests that when it comes to particularly fraught situations within culturally contested lives—such as managing participation in the cultural rubrics of both American teenage dating and religious Islam—a strategy of implicit cultural intermixing that draws on interactional ambiguity and understatement to minimize potential conflicts may prove more practically effective than a strategy of explicit cultural reconciliation that overtly articulates, and therefore draws attention to, compatibilities that are difficult to achieve.

Yusef and Salman: "Keeping It Halal"

The model of Muslim dating pursued by Yusef and Salman and their respective girlfriends—which they called "keeping it halal"—involved overt attempts to address the tensions between Islamic expectations of premarital gender relations and participation in American-style romantic relationships through explicit strategies aimed at reconciling these cultural differences. By designating Islam as an overarching framework that governed dating action, articulating religiously appropriate behavior within relationships, and emphasizing the emotional similarities between romantic and Islamic devotion, these boys sought to bring American dating practice more in line with local Islamic standards of behavior and to underscore the similarities between the two cultural frameworks while downplaying their differences. Although in the end, "keeping it halal" was dismissed as too practically challenging, for a while this model held a potent attraction for Yusef and Salman because of its apparent potential to reconcile these divergent expectations of young Muslim American life.

THE CULTURAL CLARITY OF "HALAL" DATING:
ISLAMIC FRAMEWORKS AND EXPLICIT PRACTICES

One Friday afternoon, I arranged to meet Yusef, then aged nineteen, at the mosque for Jummah prayer. We had made a plan that after prayers, I would accompany him to the ice cream parlor where he worked in the afternoon. After the prayer ended, we walked out to his car behind the mosque, hopped in, and started driving toward the suburb where he worked. As we left the city behind, passing green rolling hills in the late afternoon sunlight, Yusef seemed to relax and breathe more easily. I remembered him telling me once that he liked driving out in this area because it felt "peaceful." We sat mostly in relaxed silence, broken only when Yusef popped in a CD by the band Kings of Leon. Right after we passed beneath an overpass and headed toward another cluster of hills, he began talking:

> "One day this girl called me and she said that she liked me, you know. And I was like, 'Whoa I need to control myself.' I told her that I liked her too, because I did. And she's Muslim. But I told her that I wasn't interested in a relationship with kissing or hugging or anything like that. I just wanted to, you know, keep it halal, that's what we say. And she said that she was fine with that, that that's what she wanted, too. So we hung out all the time. That's why you never saw me at nothing for a long time. I was just hanging out with her all the time. And it kind of distracted me from everything else. My grades slipped last semester. . . . But it was incredible, you know? I had never felt that way for anyone before. Everybody around me had girlfriends, but I never knew what it was like. And I brought her to meet my Mom." I ask him, "And she was cool with that?" Yusef says, "She kept telling me, 'Don't waste your time or get distracted,' but she liked her. She's a good girl. She's a good Muslim. And she met my brothers, I mean Muhammad and Fuad, too. And she liked them and they got along."

In the model of dating exemplified by Yusef's story, one that he and the young woman he dated apparently earnestly attempted to adopt, the partners explicitly state that they will conduct the relationship in an Islamically appropriate manner ("keeping it halal") and specify limits on physical intimacy ("no kissing or hugging or anything like that"). In labeling the relationship "halal" and setting explicit rules about physical contact, Yusef and his partner tried to reconcile the competing cultural rubrics of religious Islam and American dating culture by articulating a particular relationship between the two. Specifically, practices associated with American teenage dating behavior (e.g., spending time alone together) were to be enacted within and governed by an Islamic cultural framework, as locally understood (e.g., no kissing or hugging).

Unlike Yusef, Salman, who was then only thirteen, did not actually experience a relationship defined by "keeping it halal" but did actively pursue a girl he liked in ways that emphasized a "keeping it halal" approach. Right around the time that the other Legendz started getting involved in more serious relationships, Salman met a girl named Aliyah at an ethnic festival. He got her phone number and began calling her frequently, even though he knew that she had another boyfriend. One Sunday, a week after Salman first told me about her, I was hanging out with him behind the mosque after the youth program had let out for the day. Three younger boys shot baskets on the court to our left as I stood leaning against the back wall of the building, watching Salman practice kick flips and ollies on his skateboard near the speed bump by the mosque's back door.

> "So what's up with that girl?" I ask him. "Oh," he says, looking a little taken aback. "You mean Aliyah?" "I don't know. . . . The girl you were talking about last time . . ." "Oh yeah, that's Aliyah. . . . It's pretty good." He looks down at his skateboard, then up at me again. "We're keeping it halal, you know."

Later that evening, when I asked Salman directly what he meant by that statement, he explained, "Well, it means don't just not do the haram stuff, but also do extra good things. Like teach someone and make them a better Muslim. . . . Like I've been teaching her some suras [verses from the Qur'an]."

One of the attractions of "keeping it halal" relationships is that they provide a sense of clarity to a particularly thorny cultural dilemma for young Muslims: how to date as a young practicing Muslim. If certain rules and practices of Islamic behavior could be clearly and effectively applied to American-style dating, then it might be possible to both be a properly religious young Muslim and experience the American life-course expectation of teenage dating. This possibility carried a sense of promise and relief for Yusef and Salman, and these emotions were frequently present whenever they discussed their "keeping it halal" relationships with me.

This desire for relief from the social dilemma of young Muslim dating was expressed by Salman during a conversation I had with him about a month after he first told me about Aliyah. On that particular evening, Salman and I had both attended one of the youth group's "Spiritual Nights" at the mosque. Afterward, I gave him a ride home, and we sat and chatted in the car in front of his house for a while. By this time, Salman was reaching a point of frustration in his courtship of Aliyah, both because he was receiving what he considered mixed messages from her about her interest in him and because of his own confusion over whether and how he could date in an Islamically appropriate way.

> Salman turns to me and says, "I don't really know what's going to happen. We had a fight yesterday, but then later she was saying that she wanted to dump Mike and try to make it work with me. I mean, she was even saying that she would want to try to marry me and everything." "Wow," I say. Salman says, "Yeah. I mean, that's what I wish sometimes, you know? I wish I could just say to her parents and my parents, 'We want to be together, but we're just going to keep it halal, you know?' We're not going to do anything, but just see each other and talk to each other. Then we wouldn't have to keep going through all of this."

For Salman as well as Yusef, a "keeping it halal" relationship was attractive because it held the promise of a clear plan to follow and offered a sense of cultural clarity. By applying Islamic norms to American teenage dating practice, these boys thought they might find a clear path forward, rather than a mass of multicultural confusion and ambivalence. In this way, the particular techniques the boys used to "keep it halal"—such as explicitly labeling the relationship *as* Islamic and placing limits on physical contact—served as what sociologist Dan Lainer-Vos calls "clarification practices," the cues that people use to specify the meaning of an exchange or interaction in situations of cultural ambivalence.[2] Given the uncertainty that Yusef and Salman felt in pursuing romantic relationships as young practicing Muslims, these clarification practices worked to mitigate the experienced ambiguity of the situation to some degree and provided them with the sense that there might be a potential way to date as young practicing Muslims.

In working to apply a particular set of rules to their dating lives, Yusef and Salman followed a pattern previously observed among other American teenagers, especially those growing up in conservative religious communities. Like Yusef and Salman, these young people have also worked to engage with romantic relationships in ways that would simultaneously demonstrate their continued commitment to the expectations of their religious or cultural traditions. This application of rules or labels to clarify the guiding presence of a tradition-linked morality in the midst of dating practice has been observed among young sexually active Latinas who recast safe sex as a practice in line with traditional moral "respectability," among young evangelical Christians who date "in light of Christ" or engage in "Godly dating," and among college-aged evangelical Christians who use "established rules" to keep their romantic relationships "under God's control."[3] In each of these cases, labels and rules have provided young deeply religious people with a sense of cultural and moral clarity as they entered the emotionally turbulent and culturally contested domain of teenage romantic relationships.

THE SYMBOLIC AFFINITY OF ROMANTIC LOVE AND ISLAMIC DEVOTION

In addition to designating Islam as a guiding cultural framework and specifying limits on physical intimacy, the young men who engaged in the "keeping it halal" model of dating shared a third practice in common: a consistent emphasis on the similarities between romantic teenage love and pious Islamic devotion. In the course of their relationships, Yusef and Salman regularly described their strong feelings of romantic love and their yearning to maintain Islamic standards of behavior in ways that articulated a likeness between these two emotional states. This experienced and expressed compatibility between teenage romantic emotion and Islamic ethical commitment kept these relationships and the "keeping it halal" model attractive to Yusef and Salman, even amid other challenges.

During the same car ride when Yusef told me about his dating life for the very first time, he also shared with me that the same relationship he had been so excited about had recently come to an end. He spilled his feelings on the matter:

> Yusef says, "She called me last month and said that she didn't want to do it anymore. That it was too hard. She didn't want to be disloyal to her family. That she wanted to be a good Muslim. So I was like, 'Whatever, OK. I understand what you're saying.' So now I just need to focus on my schoolwork more, and not be so distracted. I mean, I was on academic probation. My GPA slipped, so I had to go back to summer school to pick it back up." I say, "That must have been really hard when she did that. It must have hurt a lot." Yusef says, "It hurt so much, John. . . . I mean, I had never felt that way. I think I really loved her, you know. . . . I cared for her so much. And we never kissed or hugged or anything like that. Even though I wanted to kiss her sometimes or hug her or hold her hand, but I could just catch myself. But I cared for her so much. I've never cared for someone so much. Like, if she was falling, I would run to catch her. Like, if she had a scratch, I would run to get a Band-Aid and take care of it. Like, as if she was my child."

For Yusef, the emotions bound up with romantic love were closely intertwined with his expressed commitment to Islamically appropriate behavior. In this conversation, he articulated the feelings of romantic love and religious commitment at the same time and as emotionally similar. This comes across most clearly in the way in which he combined his caring feelings for this young woman ("I cared for her so much") and his sense of commitment to halal behavior ("We never kissed or hugged or anything like that"). This fusion of romantic devotion and religious devotion seemed to provide Yusef with experiential proof that both emotions could be part and parcel of one life and one activity. His perception that dating and Islamically right behavior were potentially compatible was reaffirmed later in the same conversation when he observed to me, "Now I can do it, you know? Maybe Allah wanted to show me what that was like, for five months, and now I know." Yusef's experience of halal devotion and romantic commitment as emotionally consonant allowed him to perceive and experience firsthand a compatibility between romantic and Islamic cultural rubrics.

Salman too talked about experiences of intense romantic feeling and commitment to Islamic devotion in ways that suggested their close relation to one another. Whenever Salman discussed his feelings of intimacy and closeness to Aliyah with me, his accounts were interspersed with stories of the Islamic devotion the two romantic partners shared. During one such conversation, he related:

> She was telling me that she was having these nightmares and so she wanted me to tell her *Al-Nas* [verse from the Qur'an], but I didn't know that one. So I was just teaching her the *Al-Fatiha* over the phone, and she was learning it. I'm trying to help her to be more religious. And she said it before she went to sleep and then she didn't have the nightmares anymore.

Here an expression of romantic devotion demonstrating care for a partner by helping her fall asleep was intertwined with an expression of Islamic devotion expressed by the shared memorization and recitation of suras (verses) of the Qur'an with her. As the intimate sweetness of caring for a romantic partner and the religious ritual of recitation occurred simultaneously, Salman experienced an "Islamic" form of dating as a model that made sense *in practice*, allowing both forms of devotion—to a girlfriend and to Allah—to feel similar and compatible rather than in conflict.

In seeking and experiencing some fit between their romantic and religious desires, Yusef and Salman revealed themselves to be what sociologist of religion Mark Regnerus terms "idealists"—young people who hold romanticized and somewhat unrealistic expectations of both youthful romantic relationships and religious commitments.[4] Research on highly religious young people in the United States suggests that the subset of youth who take part in abstinence pledges and modified "Christian" forms of dating tend to firmly believe (at least initially) that these idealized states of religious propriety and romantic commitment can be fully and successfully maintained at the same time, and that this belief helps motivate their initial commitment to such religious dating programs.[5] However, the same research also reveals that the vast majority of young people who attempt such programs fall short of these goals, and that "idealist" youth often come to realize that religious and romantic commitments can be extremely difficult to maintain simultaneously, especially in a context of competing cultural rubrics that set highly divergent expectations for romantic and religious lives.[6] Yusef and Salman would eventually learn this same lesson.

PRACTICAL CHALLENGES OF "KEEPING IT HALAL"

"Keeping it halal" can seem an attractive model of dating for young American Muslims because of its promise of cultural clarity and its emphasis on the symbolic affinity between romantic and religious devotions. However, at a practical level, the model's explicit designation of the style of dating as Islamically permissible (halal) and the social and cultural expectations that come with such a label can make the relationships it governs extremely challenging to maintain on a day-to-day basis. Furthermore, this model opens the partners in such relationships to criticisms and judgments from various parties that are difficult to defend. For one thing, once the arrangement is labeled "halal," any divergence from Islamic propriety can be experienced as emotionally intense and anxiety producing, even if only for the partners themselves. For example, Yusef described an interaction with his girlfriend's father, who did not know about the relationship, as follows: "He lived in Egypt for a while so he speaks Arabic. And he was talking so fast to me in Arabic, and all I could think of was,

'I'm dating your daughter.' I couldn't even look at him. I just turned away." Yusef also told me how the pair's constant self-monitoring of physical behavior became increasingly stressful and difficult over time. As noted earlier, Yusef reported that his partner experienced similar challenges as she tried to uphold a truly halal relationship, complaining to him that it was "too hard" and that she wanted to stop so that she could "be a better Muslim." As these examples illustrate, the same explicit Islamic morality that grants the "keeping it halal" relationship model its attractive sense of cultural clarity and symbolic affinity also establishes an expectation of behavior that can be nearly impossible for a contemporary urban American teenager to fully meet in practice, especially within a social context in which less restricted romantic behavior is the norm. In turn, the sense of failing to meet these self-imposed Islamic standards for behavior while dating, as well as concern about judgment for such failures from parents, community leaders, and highly religious peers, can trigger stress, guilt, and cultural confusion that can wear on the relationship itself.

Another challenge of "keeping it halal" relationships is that their explicit Islamic label, with its focus on rules and specifics, makes them easy targets of ridicule for teenage peers, including other Muslim friends who hope to align themselves with "cooler," more recognizably American ways of dating. Three months before Yusef told me about his "halal" relationship, Muhammad told me about it. But while Yusef talked about his desire to "keep it halal" with sincerity and earnest intention, Muhammed remarked on this kind of dating in teasing tones. As Muhammad and I sat behind the mosque one afternoon, I remarked that it seemed as though all the boys were suddenly getting involved with girls.

> Muhammad says, "Even Yusef!" "Really?" I ask. "Yeah," Muhammad says, "with this girl who goes to State. She's about twenty, older than him. I'm like, 'Go Yusef!' But they have like 'the halal relationship.'" I ask, "What? Like they don't do anything?" Muhammad smiles and says, "No. They just . . . like, they just shake hands. I'm not sure they even do a high five."

Because "keeping it halal" dating involves overt labeling and explicit specification of rules for behavior, this model and its stated guidelines are visible to close peers and therefore available as a target for ridicule. Here, Muhammad's mockery of the "keeping it halal" approach was centrally focused on this specific, rule-concerned aspect of "keeping it halal" ("I'm not even sure they do a high five"). The practice of poking fun at peers who try to date in too "religious" a fashion—a tendency also evident among various groups of American Christian youth[7]—adds further pressure to teens who try to "keep it halal." Along with broader youth culture and hormonal desires, this subtle peer criticism can further work to push young "idealists" like Yusef and Salman away from the models of explicitly Islamic dating they initially find attractive and toward more understated and subtle strategies of dating as a Muslim American youth.

Abdul, Muhammad, and Fuad: Dating While Muslim

Abdul, Muhammad, and Fuad started seriously dating girls at around the same time Yusef and Salman did, at the ages of eighteen, nineteen, and sixteen, respectively. Their relationships involved the same expressions of romantic enthusiasm, time spent with particular young women, and occasional hiding of information from parents that characterized the relationships of the other boys. In contrast to Yusef and Salman, though, these young men did not associate their dating practices with an explicitly Islamic moral program. To the contrary, Abdul, Muhammad, and Fuad actively *avoided* articulating a specific relationship between Islamic standards of behavior and their own romantic relationships, even though their dating did incorporate both recognizably American and locally Islamic cultural elements. Rather than promising to "keep it halal," Abdul, Muhammad, and Fuad engaged in what I call "dating while Muslim," that is, dating in a way that reflects involvement in both Islamic and American youth cultural rubrics but avoids explicitly labeling either rubric as such or attempting to define a specific relationship between the two.

Through three core practices—decentering Islamic discourse, resisting specificity, and engaging in implicitly Muslim courting—Abdul,

Muhammad, and Fuad maintained religious Islam's *presence* within their everyday dating lives while mitigating its restrictiveness regarding their American teenage dating behavior. First, the boys incorporated Islamic terms and cultural elements into their dating, but in ways that were marginal rather than central to the meaning of these interactions. Second, they regularly referred to notions of haram (forbidden) or halal (permissible) in relation to their dating practice, but did so in ways that purposefully avoided specifying which acts of dating behavior fell into which category. Finally, they engaged in courtship practices drawn from and associated with their Muslim community, but in ways that downplayed rather than emphasized the identification of these practices as "Islamic." In this way, they attempted to participate in both American teenage dating behavior and locally Islamic behavior while avoiding an explicit application of local Islamic standards to their dating practices. As will be seen, the implicit and understated nature of "dating while Muslim" carried certain social advantages within the Legendz's culturally contested context, and the boys who followed this model seemed to experience more easily maintained and less anxiety-prone romantic relationships.

DECENTERING ISLAMIC DISCOURSE IN DATING

In contrast to Yusef and Salman, who tried to explicitly integrate discourses of Islamic morality into their American dating practice, the young men who "dated while Muslim" pursued romantic relationships without overtly applying the standards of Islamic religiosity to their own dating behavior. Rather than establishing a set of Islamic principles to guide their behavior within romantic relationships, Abdul, Muhammad, and Fuad treated Islamic religious discourse as a set of terms, practices, and references that were proximate and relevant but never central or defining elements of their romantic endeavors. In fact, they often spoke about their emerging relationships with no reference to Islamic morality or behavioral expectations whatsoever.

This central difference between Abdul, Muhammad, and Fuad and the "keeping it halal" boys was most evident in the way in which these young men talked about their developing relationships. Like the others, these three expressed enthusiasm about their girlfriends and their first "in love" relationships. But while Yusef's and Salman's expressions of romantic excitement were inflected with Islamic language and expectations of "halal" behavior, the articulations of young love voiced by the "dating while Muslim" boys were utterly lacking in such Islamic moral idealism. In the early stages of his relationship with a young woman named Eman, for example, Abdul spoke about her using idealizing romantic language:

> "I mean, she has everything. She's smart, you know? She's a good person, she's like everything at the same time."
> "I'm gonna marry Eman, and Fuad's gonna marry Leila."
> "Is this for your book, John O'Brien? Put this in your book, John: I found the perfect girl."

When Abdul, Muhammad, and Fuad did refer to religiously Islamic ideas or expressions in relation to their romantic relationships, they did so in a way that differed from that adopted by those who were "keeping it halal." While the discourse of the latter suggested the compatibility of romantic love and local understandings of proper Islamic behavior, the "dating while Muslim" youth celebrated the perfection of their relationships in language that generally emphasized the concerns of secularized romance but also drew on familiar Islamic symbols to express gratitude for and excitement about these romantic experiences. This difference in the two groups' ways of articulating romantic relationships became evident one evening as I drove with Abdul and Fuad on our way back from a fundraising event at Abdul's girlfriend's suburban school. In this particular conversation, we were discussing how girlfriends could differ in terms of whether they held "positive" versus "negative" attitudes toward life and the world. Specifically, we were comparing one of Abdul's ex-girlfriends, Noor, to his current girlfriend, Eman.

> "That girl Noor was like that, too," Abdul says. "Like what?" I ask. He says, "She was just negative about everything. . . . And I really started to get sick of it, and then she got mad at me." I say,

"Eman isn't like that at all." "I know," Abdul says. "That's why I really love her." "Yeah," Fuad says, overlapping with Abdul, "you shouldn't stay with someone who is just negative all the time." "Yeah, Eman doesn't seem like that," I say. Abdul looks back and says, "Yeah, Fuad, we got some good ones!" "Alhamdulillah [Praise be to God]," Fuad says. "*Insha'Allah* [If God wills it]," Abdul says. "Insha'Allah," Fuad says.

In this excerpt of excited conversation, Fuad and Abdul expressed enthusiasm for their girlfriends using Arabic and Islamic language, thanking God for their emerging relationships ("Alhamdulillah"), and articulating the wish that their good fortune continue if so willed by God ("Insha'Allah"). Such references to religious Islam in a dating context differed significantly from those I heard from Yusef and Salman. For them, Islam was present as a centrally integrated, guiding framework for behavior, a way of "keeping it halal." For the "dating while Muslim" youth, in contrast, Islam was present as an assortment of symbols on which they might draw for expressive purposes or to comment on the principal action but that were never meant to suggest that the relationship was fundamentally subject to the rules of Islamically halal behavior.

Part of the practical logic of "dating while Muslim," then, was to keep religious Islam *relevant* in dating interactions; after all, these youth still wished to present themselves as "good Muslims" to each other and potential romantic partners, yet without suggesting that Islam had to be adopted as a guiding framework for the entire relationship or somehow explicitly reconciled with the expectations of teenage dating. One way to achieve this aim was by demonstrating one's *ability* to use Islamic terms and practices in a dating situation without suggesting that such schemas should or would be applied to the relationship *in general*. The boys recounted one example of this treatment of Islam as a relevant but not dominant system of meaning on a particularly exciting night when Abdul, Muhammad, Fuad, and Tariq went to visit a girl in whom Abdul was interested and met her family at her home. Later that same night, Abdul—who was eighteen at the time—told me how they had arrived at the large suburban home before the girl's parents had returned from running errands. The young woman, Eman, and her sister Zeynep, had invited the four boys to sit in the large family room and wait for their parents.

> ABDUL: And I was really nervous, because I've never met a girlfriend's parents or the parents of a girl I was talking to. . . . It was just awkward. Then Muhammad was cracking some jokes, and then it was quiet for a while. You know, I was uncomfortable, and so I was very quiet. Then her older sister, Sala, puts *Glee* on the TV. And I was thinking, "Uh, I really don't like this show. I hate it actually." [He laughs.]
>
> JOHN: Then what happened?
>
> ABDUL: Then you know what song they were singing on *Glee*? "The Thong Song."
>
> JOHN: Seriously?
>
> ABDUL: [laughing] Yeah. So then it felt more awkward, and everyone was being all quiet, so I said . . . "Astaghfirullah!" ["God forgive us!"]
>
> JOHN: Really?
>
> ABDUL: And her sister laughed, and she laughed, and everyone laughed. It sort of broke the ice.
>
> JOHN: Why do you think you said that?
>
> ABDUL: [pausing] I felt like I had to say something. . . . I had to be cool with everyone, you know. . . . You do something with religion to feel accepted . . . something you can relate to.

This interaction involved practices and behaviors commonly associated with the early stage of flirtation in an average American teenage dating relationship: A young man comes to visit a young woman in whom he has a romantic interest in the company of his and her friends. They talk and spend time together with adults nearby but not immediately present. He's nervous.

In this case, the sexual content of the television show added to the interaction's sense of romantic and sensual possibility. Despite the fact that this worldly and sexually explicit pop culture did not seem to create visible trouble for any of those present, Abdul made a brief statement asking for Allah's forgiveness ("Astaghfirullah!") for witnessing such profane material. The others laughed, and Abdul was able to demonstrate his *familiarity* with the tools of Islamic morality without suggesting that the evening's behavior—or the potential fledging relationship—should or need be conducted in a thoroughly "Islamic" manner. As he tried "to be cool with everyone," he demonstrated that while religiously Islamic perspectives on profane material and behaviors could and might be taken into account in the course of the relationship, they did not need to be treated as central or defining elements of the arrangement.

RESISTING A SPECIFICITY OF HARAM AND HALAL

A second way in which Abdul, Fuad, and Muhammad maintained the relevance of religious Islam in their dating lives while mitigating its power to define their relationships was by invoking the designations of halal (permissible) and haram (forbidden) in reference to physical intimacy, even as they actively avoided specifics as to what kind of behavior belonged in which category. While those working to "keep it halal" set specific and explicit limits on physical intimacy, those who were "dating while Muslim" avoided any clarification of particular dos and don'ts of physical intimacy, instead using "halal" and "haram" in ways that allowed room for definitional ambiguity and potentially diverse behaviors within a relationship. I witnessed such a usage of these terms one Sunday afternoon at the mosque when I walked out the back door of the building to find Tariq (then sixteen), Fuad (then also sixteen), and some other kids sitting on the bleachers near the basketball court and talking to an older boy named Mustafa.

> Mustafa says, "I mean, the thing about relationships is, I think it's only the business of those people in the relationship, you know?" I nod. Mustafa says, "You can have a relationship. It's fine, as long as you don't do anything that isn't halal, you know?" The boys nod. Tariq says, "As long as you have the intention to marry the person, it's OK, right?" Mustafa nods, "Yeah, and it's haram to

have sex before marriage." Fuad jumps in quickly: "Man, I never had the intention to have sex before marriage!" Mustafa says, "As long as you do it in the right way, you know, you have your homeys around. You don't be alone with just that person [he gestures to an invisible someone next to him], so nothing happens, you know." Fuad says, as if checking his own behavior against this criteria, "Yeah, Abdul's always with us . . . and her older sister's always with us, too." Tariq asks, "What if it's *her* homeys that are with you?" "Her homeys?" Mustafa asks. "Yeah, that's OK, too." He continues, "As long as you don't do anything that it says in the Qur'an not to do, it's OK to have relationships."

This was the only conversation I ever witnessed among Tariq, Fuad, Abdul, and Muhammad in which they came close to considering the specifics of physically intimate acts and their status vis-à-vis Islamic morality. And even in this discussion, any details—save the specific ruling that sex before marriage is haram—were completely absent. Instead, unspecified pronouns were used: "Don't do *anything* that isn't halal"; "Don't do *anything* that it says in the Qur'an not to do." In this way, any *particular* acts of physical intimacy—kissing, holding hands, anything more serious—were left unnamed and therefore un-evaluated in terms of Islamic standards for behavior. Some level of physical intimacy between these boys and their partners was implied in the conversation; they were, after all, discussing what you could and could not do with your girlfriend. The fact that particular acts were largely left unspecified, however, along with the invocation of the categories of haram and halal, allowed the boys to temporarily inhabit a social space in which they could be reasonably considered as both participants in legitimate teenage romantic relationships who might do "things" with their girlfriends and conscientious young Muslims concerned with the Islamic propriety of their behavior.

Abdul, Fuad, Muhammad, and some of their friends consistently strove to maintain this kind of strategic ambiguity when discussing the physical aspects of their romantic relationships. This jointly constructed interactional ambiguity—in which details of physical intimacy were never explicitly stated, but the *possibility* of their occurrence was suggested—allowed the boys to present themselves as involved in a legitimate (i.e., physically intimate) teenage dating relationship while simultaneously withholding any particular evidence that overtly connected them to clearly haram behavior. I witnessed another instance of this interactional ambiguity one Friday evening as Abdul and I dropped Tariq (then seventeen) off at a movie theater where he was going to meet his girlfriend and some of her friends.

> Tariq says, "You can just drop me off here, cuz I'm going to that theater over there." I pull over and he hops out. "OK, see you later," he says. "Have a good time," I say. "Yeah," Abdul says, in an ironic tone. "Keep it halal." Tariq laughs, "Alright," and hops out of the car and walks across the street.

Abdul's reminder to Tariq to "keep it halal" as he prepared to spend time with his girlfriend was delivered in an ironic and knowing tone, suggesting that both of the boys were aware that Tariq's behavior while at the movie might not fall completely within the bounds of Islamic propriety. At the same time and equally importantly, Tariq did not acknowledge that he would act inappropriately, and no direct references to specific acts of physical intimacy were made. As a result, the ambiguity of the situation—constructed by Abdul's ironic tone and the lack of specifics regarding acts of physical intimacy—allowed two potential realities to exist at once: that Tariq would act outside the lines of Islamically appropriate behavior and that he would not do so but instead would maintain a halal standard of conduct. The presence of the term "halal" bestowed an air of Islamic propriety and ethical consideration onto the proceedings, but the ironic tone and lack of detail prevented the possibility of judging any actual dating behavior from the perspective of Islamic morality.

This kind of discursive ambiguity about sexual activity is actually quite common among young people in the United States more broadly. The vagueness of the term "hooking up," for example, prevents young men from having to disclose to peers whether or not they have in fact had sexual intercourse with a female partner, while they often hope that their male friends will interpret this term to mean that they have.[8] For young men who "date while Muslim," the vagueness of the discussion about "keeping it halal" similarly does double duty, allowing two possible and desirable realities to remain in play: that they are dating in a suitably "Islamic" way and not engaging in physical intimacy at all, and that they are dating in a suitably "American" way and engaging in some level of physical intimacy with their partner. Among the Legendz, the repeated invocation of the category of halal without any specification of its contents allowed the boys to demonstrate a familiarity with and symbolic connection to the locally salient cultural rubric of Islamic religiosity and morality without limiting the possibilities of engaging in the rubric of American dating, including the practice of particular and unnamed teenage dating behaviors.

MAINTAINING A LOW-KEY AND UNMARKED ISLAMIC PROPRIETY

Although Fuad, Muhammad, and Abdul resisted defining their dating efforts as fundamentally "Islamic" and avoided specifying details of potentially halal or haram behavior, they conducted their relationships in ways that most members of their peer group and religious community would have recognized as consistent with the core standards of proper premarital Islamic courtship. They talked about, and as far as I could tell, followed through with abstaining from sexual intercourse. They spent time getting to know and trying to win the approval of their girlfriends' parents. And they pursued relationships exclusively with Muslim young women. In contrast to those who worked to "keep it halal," these young men engaged in dating practices that aligned with certain communal expectations of Islamic behavior but *understated* rather than called attention to the congruence between their own actions and an overarching Islamic morality or Muslim communal norm.

When these members of the Legendz spoke about their commitment to abstain from having sex before marriage, they incorporated this decision into the flow of everyday conversation and banter rather than setting it aside as a declaration that merited special attention or religious language. The matter was often treated in conversation as a basic, if annoying, fact of life. One late night after I accompanied the boys to one of their hip hop performances across town, we returned to their neighborhood and stopped at a Mexican fast food place to get something to eat before parting ways. After we sat down with our tacos and chicken, I heard Abdul, who was sitting across from me, murmur something along the lines of the following to Muhammad:

> "That's why you're a virgin." A few minutes later Abdul says it to Muhammad again: "That's why you're a virgin." Abdul asks me, "John, are you a virgin?" I give him a comically confused look, as I know that he knows that I'm married and my wife is pregnant. "How could he be a virgin?" Muhammad says. "His wife is having a baby." "I hope I'm not a virgin," I say. They laugh. Abdul says, "Cuz you know, we have to wait until we get married." He says this in a mock-annoyed tone, and rolls his eyes a little.

The same attitude toward premarital celibacy—that it was a taken-for-granted, if annoying, feature of their lives—came up in every conversation I had with the boys on this topic. Once Muhammad told me that he thought Salman wanted to have a girlfriend only "because of what he sees other people do who have girlfriends," which I understood to mean having sex. But then he added, "But we're not like that." Similarly, the weekend after a youth program retreat at which Omar approached some of the boys about dating, Fuad told me that the religious director had later spoken to his girlfriend's mother about what was happening:

> "And what did her mom say?" I ask. He says, "She was telling Leila that we had to keep ourselves under control." I nod. He says, "That's what Omar was saying, too. You know, no sex before marriage. I mean, of course [he shrugs and laughs]. I know that. . . . Omar thinks that's the only reason we want to have girlfriends is to have sex."

One way to interpret these statements about premarital sexual abstention is by reasoning that the boys were only saying this for my benefit, performing a more moral Muslim self before another

Muslim adult. Yet two observations challenge this claim. First, the boys became comfortable making innuendos about and even engaging in physical intimacy with their girlfriends in my presence, so they certainly were not attempting to present themselves as perfectly moral to me. Second, in one instance Fuad made this kind of statement about abstinence to Abdul when I was not meant to hear. On that particular afternoon, I was shooting baskets with Muhammad while Fuad and Abdul sat and talked on the bleachers. At one point, the ball bounced off my foot and rolled near the guys sitting down. As I passed them to pick it up, I heard Fuad concluding a conversation with Abdul.

> As I get there, Fuad finishes saying something to Abdul. Abdul laughs, looks at me, and says, "John, you have to put that line in the book!" "What did he say?" I ask. Abdul looks at Fuad expectantly. Fuad says, "I said I need to find a girlfriend who can commit to me but doesn't mind waiting until marriage." "Oh," I say. Abdul laughs: "You need to write that down."

While Yusef and Salman treated premarital abstinence as something worthy of and symbolically compatible with explicitly Islamic declarations of moral purity and commitment, the other boys' approach was stylistically understated, or low key, and therefore less charged with high-stakes expectations of religiously appropriate behavior. For Fuad, Muhammad, and Abdul, abstention from sex before marriage was an ingrained and generally accepted fact of their social situation, a cultural expectation that was part of the everyday logistics of a teenage romantic relationship.

A second communally accepted approach to premarital courtship that this subset of boys incorporated into their dating practices in an understated way was the attempt to get to know and win the approval of their potential girlfriends' parents and other family members. While this is certainly not a practice unique to Muslim American immigrant communities, it was something that the boys did because it made their relationships feel more "appropriate" to them. Abdul, for example, felt strongly about meeting his girlfriend's parents before they ever went out together. One night, Abdul and the other boys visited the home of Abdul's girlfriend's family in the suburb of Greenmont. The meeting went well, and as I drove home with the boys in Muhammad's car, Muhammad asked Abdul why we had ended up spending time at her family's home.

> Muhammad says, "Abdul, I thought we were supposed to go to a movie or something." "We were going to," Abdul says. "But I said to her that I thought I should meet her parents first. And she was like, 'Well, I don't know if we're ready for that.' And that made me feel kind of bad, like, 'Oh, you don't think we're ready for that?'"

Abdul treated meeting his prospective girlfriend's parents as something he "should" do, but he neither talked about the choice in a way that linked it to Islamic morality—even though it was something that mosque leaders repeatedly told the young people they should do when pursuing premarital relationships—nor expressed it in terms of strong emotions of guilt or halal versus haram behavior. In other words, even though such a meeting was a practice consonant with local standards of Islamic behavior, it was conducted in a way completely free of references to religious Islam.

A third practice that aligned with communal expectations of premarital courtship and was incorporated into these boys' low-key version of "dating while Muslim" was their selection of exclusively Muslim girlfriends. Parents and mosque adults repeatedly stressed to youth that they should marry other Muslims. As was seen previously, those who engaged in "keeping it halal" dating emphasized and highlighted the Muslim identity and religious standing of their romantic partners. Fuad, Muhammad, and Abdul also only dated young Muslim women, but for them the experience was not about a shared religious devotion or jointly declared Islamic morality but rather having someone else who was socially positioned to understand and co-navigate the experience of dating in a way that was "Muslim" but interpreted that label in a low-key manner. What this meant in practice was that these boys chose to date Muslim girls who, like them, could pay heed to and reference jointly recognized Islamic moral standards but also preferred a low-key and flexible, rather than explicit and restrictive, approach to religious propriety.

The Muslim American identity of their girlfriends was meaningful to these boys because it meant that these young women were people who were familiar with and could therefore be joint partners in navigating the subtle negotiations of dating as young Muslims in urban America. Once in such relationships, this joint navigation often came to serve as a basis of shared experience and identity between romantic partners. The ways in which two young people could effectively negotiate the subtleties of this arrangement relied in part on their partners' common identity as Muslim American youth and their consequent familiarity with this culturally contested situation. Jokes about and references to this experience of negotiating the competing cultural rubrics of American teenage dating and proper Islamic behavior reinforced feelings of friendship and closeness between romantic partners and among the circle of friends engaged in this kind of dating practice.

Even as they spent time together as romantic pairs, such couples would often tease each other and their friends from an "Islamic" perspective, saying things like, "Would your mother approve of that?" if another couple was holding hands and shaking their head ruefully and proclaiming, "Haram!" if two friends hugged one another. Key to the logic of these situations was all participants' familiarity with both cultural rubrics at play. While the Muslimness of the girlfriends in the "keeping it halal" model was partly an attempt by those boys and their partners to craft an Islamically pure relationship, in the context of a "dating while Muslim" relationship, this identification served as a basis for understanding and jointly navigating a shared and tricky cultural experience. In this way, those who "dated while Muslim" assumed a low-key approach to dating as a Muslim teenager, one that fully and openly acknowledged the complexity of the situation but made no attempt to reach a full reconciliation of these different cultural perspectives in practice.

Conclusion: Patterns in the Legendz's Dating Practices

This chapter has detailed two distinct models through which members of the Legendz attempted to reconcile the contradictions between Islamic expectations of premarital gender relations and their participation in American-style teenage romantic relationships. Yusef and Salman sought to manage this dilemma by articulating and pursuing an overtly Islamic approach to dating, which the boys called "keeping it halal." As practiced by Yusef and Salman with their partners, "keeping it halal" entailed an explicit labeling of their romantic activity as Islamically appropriate (halal) as well as a stated commitment to setting specific limits on physical intimacy. This approach was initially attractive to these young men because it promised a level of cultural clarity and emphasized an attractive similarity between states of romantic love and Islamic piety. These factors in turn allowed Yusef and Salman to experience a pleasing, aesthetic overlap between normally conflicting cultural rubrics in the early stages of their relationships. While "keeping it halal" worked well as an articulated aspiration and an initial guide for young Muslim Americans' behavior while dating in America, its effectiveness as a lasting strategy for reconciling teenage dating and Islamic morality eventually fell short for those who attempted it.

Exemplifying an alternative approach to managing the dilemma of dating as a young Muslim, Abdul, Muhammad, and Fuad *avoided* articulating their dating relationships within an explicitly Islamic moral framework or by setting clear boundaries on physical intimacy. Instead, they emphasized the aspects of their relationships that aligned with a culture of romantic love (e.g., the perfection of their partners, fidelity, plans for the future) while trying to keep Islamic understandings present but marginal and the possibility of physical intimacy alive but obscure by discussing such subjects in strategically ambiguous ways. Although these boys engaged in courting practices associated with good Muslim behavior by their community (e.g., getting to know their partners' parents, abstaining from premarital sex, and choosing Muslim partners), they did so in ways that downplayed rather than called attention to the "Islamic" nature of these practices. The "dating while Muslim" model thus seemed to place less overt ethical pressure on Abdul, Muhammad, and Fuad while still allowing them to feel and appear connected to their cultural and religious community.

What social factors might help explain which of the young men pursued which dating strategy? Given the small number of young men in my sample of dating Muslims, it would be impossible for me to definitively determine the effects of variables such as age, ethnicity, and religiosity on a particular boy's choice of strategy. However, with the evidence at my disposal, I feel that I can make a prima facie case for why Yusef and Salman attempted to "keep it halal" while the others did not. One possible explanation lies in their ethnic and cultural backgrounds. It might be the case, for example, that young men raised within certain cultural traditions are taught to think differently (or not to think at all) about the possibilities for dating as a young Muslim. But this explanation is not borne out by these boys' dating patterns. The two Jordanian Legendz, Yusef and Abdul (who were actually brothers), followed different approaches to dating, as did the two South Asian Legendz, Tariq and Salman. Although the Sudanese brothers both shared a "dating while Muslim" approach, I think this commonality is best explained by their sharing the same relatively liberal mother, whom I saw take a somewhat lax approach to her sons' involvement with young women, rather than by some characteristic of Sudanese culture more generally.

A second possible explanation for the choice of dating strategy among the Legendz is age. It might be the case, for example, that the further along a young man is in adolescent development, the more effectively he will have been socialized into the morals of his mosque community and religious family, and the more likely he will be to try to "keep it halal." Alternatively, it may be possible that greater age is correlated with greater independence of thought and desire for autonomy among young men, which might lead an older boy to attempt to "date while Muslim" in order to create some distance between himself and communal and religious restrictions. While both explanations seem plausible, neither one sufficiently fits my findings, as the set who "dated while Muslim" included young men in the "middle range" of the adolescent age spectrum—Abdul and Tariq were both sixteen, while Muhammad was nineteen—while the "keeping it halal" set included both the second-oldest (Yusef, at nineteen) and the youngest (Salman, at thirteen) members of the group. In my view, this is not a clear enough pattern to establish age as the central factor in the choice of dating strategy.

I believe that the difference in choice of dating strategy is best explained by the centrality of religiosity to a given young person's sense of self and identity. While each of the Legendz considered himself a practicing Muslim, attempted to fulfill the basic tenets of the religion, and attended the mosque regularly, not all of them did so to the same degree and with the same level of enthusiasm. In my observation, of all of the Legendz, it was Yusef and Salman, the two youth who followed the "keeping it halal" model of dating, who were the most consistently concerned with maintaining the identity of a deeply religious young Muslim and presenting this identity effectively to others. Yusef's identity as a "good" Muslim was consistently central to and visible in his everyday life. Mosque leaders often asked him to perform the call to prayer, he frequently reminded other young people of prayers or other religious duties, and adults and youth at the mosque regularly and warmly called him by the nickname "the imam." Salman, though much younger, exhibited a strikingly similar pattern with respect to his religious identity. He often boasted that his father regularly performed the call to prayer at the mosque, spoke of reading the Qur'an and reciting suras at home, and was frequently concerned with praying enough and on time.

It seems to me that the centrality to Yusef's and Salman's identities of being and appearing as "good," deeply religious Muslims made "keeping it halal" an appealing mode of dating for both of them, but less so for the other Legendz, for two reasons. First, and perhaps most obviously, the overtly Islamic framework of this kind of dating made it more suitable for a more deeply religious young person. Since the "keeping it halal" mode symbolically places Islamic religiosity front and center, it is well suited to a young person who values his or her own religious identity because such a religiously cast model of romantic relationship causes a minimum of disruption to their sense of themselves as adequately pious. For Yusef and Salman, this seemed to be part of the attraction of "keeping it halal." This appeal could be seen in the early stages of these young men's relationships in their articulated appreciation of their ability to blend religious and romantic experiences and to feel like they were living out both Islamic and teenage dating lives.

But there may be a second, more subtle, reason for Yusef's and Salman's attraction to "keeping it halal." As discussed earlier, these young men not only were concerned with their religious identities but also thought about religious as well as romantic endeavors in an extremely "idealistic" way. Like some young people in other conservative religious communities, their expectations for perfection in their religious practice were equally as high as their expectations for perfection in their romantic relationships. While such idealism, or possibly naiveté, seems more obviously fitting in the case of Salman, who was only thirteen at the time, it also suited the character of Yusef, who claimed to have had almost no experience with young women prior to this period, and whose sweet, innocent sincerity regarding matters religious and romantic was striking for a nineteen-year-old. In contrast, Muhammad, Abdul, Fuad, and Tariq were less invested in highly religious identities and were also more experienced in terms of relationships. For the boys who were more "worldly," the "dating while Muslim" approach, which offered greater flexibility for the potential pushing of boundaries, seemed to prove more attractive and effective.

Based on my observations, relationships in the "dating while Muslim" mode appeared to be generally more compatible with and suitable for the particular culturally contested context in which the Legendz found themselves. By emphasizing romantic love independently from Islamic moral perfection, maintaining strategic ambiguity with respect to physical intimacy, and adopting a low-key approach to communally approved courtship practices, Fuad, Muhammad, and Abdul appeared to take a more sustainable and less stressful approach to dating as Muslims than did Yusef and Salman. By keeping the relationship between religious Islam and their dating practice understated and undefined, those who "dated while Muslim" seemed to effectively reduce the potentially negative effects of cultural tensions between Islamic and American teenage dating expectations.

Further evidence of the continued local preference for "dating while Muslim" was the fact that as time went by, the young men who had previously worked to "keep it halal" began adopting this more implicit approach to Muslim youth dating. In April 2010, right before I left the mosque, I learned that Yusef (who was then almost twenty) was involved in a second romantic relationship, this time with a girl named Amal, and was conducting it in a way that looked and sounded a lot more like "dating while Muslim" than "keeping it halal." In brief conversations at the mosque, he told me about Amal, saying that he had met her parents and that she was Muslim, but he never mentioned anything about an explicit approach to halal behavior in the relationship the way he had with his previous girl-friends. One evening at the mosque, I had the opportunity to speak with him further about this subject. On that particular night, Yusef and I were sitting across from each other at a white folding table up in the youth room while both of us did schoolwork on our laptops. After a while, we took a break and I asked him how things were going with Amal. He told me that everything was going "really great" and that she was "the coolest person." Since I was wondering how he was approaching this relationship with regard to Islamic propriety, I asked him directly.

> "So are you guys, like, keeping it halal?" I look down at my shoe, then over at him. "Weeeeell . . ." he says, rolling his eyes upward, and smiling a little. "We're trying to, but sometimes things get a little out of control. . . . It's hard when you like someone like that. But, you know, we try to keep it chill. When we start to do something, like kissing or something, we try to calm ourselves down and say, OK, we don't want this to get too out of hand. We were just talking about that the other day."

From this statement, it was clear that Yusef had moved toward the "dating while Muslim" model, in which the concept of halal was considered and acknowledged but not applied as an overarching framework. Rather than explicitly defining the relationship as a primarily Islamic endeavor from the outset, Yusef and Amal were making an effort to incorporate the cultural tension between Muslim propriety and American teenage dating into the relationship itself, as a shared project of the romantic partners. As a result, they were experiencing the relationship as a *manageable challenge* rather than a stressful test, an *ongoing and imperfect project* rather than a zero-sum game. Through the intentional, strategic maintenance of ambiguity, concrete practices of decentering discourse, resistance to specificity, and a downplaying of explicitly "Islamic" cultural action, young Muslims like Yusef worked to keep multiple cultural rubrics at play, seeking the subjective experience of both religious Islam and American youth dating culture while trying not to feel overly constrained or fully defined by either one.

5

On Being a Muslim in Public

A Troubled Public Identity

It's a sunny Sunday afternoon in mid-October, and the parking lot just behind the City Mosque is bustling with people and activity. Today is the mosque's annual "Walk-a-Thon and Carnival Fundraiser," and to mark the occasion small plastic triangular flags colored bright green, blue, yellow, and white have been strung along the building's back wall. Parents and other adult volunteers sit around a dozen or so square, white folding tables set up in the lot, selling jewelry, colorful scarves, samosas, and Islamic DVDs and CDs, as well as sodas, cotton candy, and popcorn to the kids and parents milling around. The smell of grilled hamburgers wafts across the lot from where Yusef is stationed behind the mosque's large barbecue. Although the "walk-a-thon" ended several hours ago, about eighty people of various ages are still hanging around, chatting and catching up with one another, trying their hand at makeshift carnival games assembled by the Sunday School teachers, and checking out the various wares for sale at the tables. Many of them wear the bright white and orange "City Mosque Walk-a-Thon" T-shirts that were made for the event.

I'm stationed behind one of the white folding tables, sitting alongside youth program members Nailah, Sana, and Muhammad. Our official task is twofold: to inform people about the youth program's upcoming "open house" scheduled for the following weekend and to sell some of the many surplus Muslim Youth Program T-shirts that have accumulated in the back of the program's office over the last few years. To this end, our table is set up with a stack of brightly colored flyers for next week's event alongside neatly folded samples of the three MYP T-shirts on offer today. The first shirt is dark blue and simply features the word "FAITH" in large white block letters across its front. The second is a play on the five-bar icon indicating reception level on cell phones. This symbol appears in white on the front of the maroon shirt, while the message on the back reads: "Muslim Youth Program: Raising the Bar." The third shirt is neon green and features a parody of the Apple logo with the word "iMuslim" in white beneath it.

Three African American–looking women sit in a cluster of chairs to the right of our table. They talk and laugh with one another, sipping coffee from paper cups. The woman nearest us, who wears glasses and her white hair pulled back in a bun, looks over at the shirts and says with interest, "These shirts are pretty nice." Standing up and stepping closer to the table, she inspects the shirts more carefully. "I like this one that says 'faith,'" she remarks. She looks over the other two shirts and then turns back toward the other two women, who have also stood up and edged closer to the table. "But I don't want it to say 'Muslim' on it," she says to them. "Because, you know, with all the stuff going on in the world, people will look at me like I'm crazy." Her two friends nod sympathetically. Nailah, Sana, and Muhammad are sitting farther from the woman than I am, so I can't tell whether or not they hear her comment. The woman leans over the table and picks up the "Faith" shirt. She repeats, more audibly this time and facing us, "I think I might get this, but I don't want anything that says 'Muslim' on it." She turns her attention to the next shirt. "Like, I like this, 'Muslims Raising the Bar,' but I don't want it to say Muslim. You know? Because people will look at me like I'm crazy."

Nailah has moved closer to attend to this potential customer, and a different woman listening in on the conversation to the left of our table leans over and says quietly to me, "Well, you can't hide all the time, either."

The first woman is still looking carefully at the "Faith" T-shirt. Nailah speaks to her, trying to make a sale: "Well *that one* doesn't say Muslim on it."

Looking at the back of the shirt, the woman asks, "MYP—what's that?"

Sana says, "Muslim Youth Program," and points to a sign by the table.

"Oh," the woman replies, then asks, "Do you have any long-sleeved shirts?"

"We have a few upstairs, but they're just from the ski trip," Nailah says. "Is that OK?" The woman shrugs, and Nailah asks Muhammad to go up and get them.

As we wait, I ask the woman, "So why do you not want to buy it if it says 'Muslim'?"

She says, "You know, with the terrorism going on . . . if I have a shirt that says 'Muslim' or, like that one"—pointing to one of the Walk-a-Thon shirts, "'City Mosque,' people will look at me like I'm crazy, and they might say something, and then I might have to punch them. And I don't want to get into that kind of a situation."

"Oh," I nod.

Muhammad comes out the back door of the mosque with the ski trip shirt. After looking it over, the older woman says that she "doesn't like the markings" and decides not to buy it after all. She places it back on the table and turns back to join her friends.

———

This Muslim American woman's hesitation to buy and wear a shirt that would overtly label her as a Muslim exemplifies an ongoing predicament faced by most members of the City Mosque community: whether and how to present themselves as Muslims in public social life. A central concern among Muslims living in twenty-first-century America is the ever-present possibility that a public revelation of one's Muslim identity could lead to undesirable outcomes such as stigmatization, discrimination, or harassment.[1] While negative consequences of revealing or asserting one's Muslim identity in public are certainly not guaranteed (even the concerned woman at the mosque said only that people "might" say something), mosque members consistently consider the *possibility* of their occurrence. Therefore, various strategies for presenting oneself as a Muslim in public are discussed, evaluated, adjusted, and adopted among community members.

This chapter explores the practical puzzle of publicly presenting oneself as a Muslim in a climate of potential harassment and analyzes two identifiable but diverging methods for managing this vexing social dilemma adopted within the City Mosque community. While the Legendz's method consisted of presenting what I call a "low-key Islam" in public, demonstrating American teenage capabilities, and displaying their agency and autonomy, mosque leaders promoted a method that involved foregrounding one's Islamic identity, demonstrating a noble vulnerability to discrimination, and appealing to non-Muslims for sympathy. Although for the most part, these methods were able to coexist side by side with little conflict, over time the differences between them grew more apparent and eventually revealed a significant and meaningful fracture at the heart of the City Mosque community.

The Legendz's Method for Being Muslim in Public

The Legendz's method for presenting a Muslim identity in public was shaped by the particular cultural milieu of their teenage social world, which included a mix of rejection and acceptance by non-Muslim peers, expectations of "cool" masculine and stereotypically African American–associated behavior in their schools and neighborhoods, and exposure to media that promoted youth culture activities and notions of individualistic action. Over time, these cultural elements and experiences were absorbed, adopted, recombined, and refined within the social space of their small friendship group. What emerged was a relatively stable and consistent method for presenting a Muslim self in public, one that strongly resonated with the central tenets of the Legendz's small-group identity. In fact, the three practices that constituted the core of the Legendz's method for presenting a public Muslim identity strongly resemble the in-group cultural strategies discussed in earlier chapters.

The Legendz's method involved, first, the presentation of an identifiably Muslim self in a way that simultaneously downplayed the centrality of Islam to this identity, or a style of self-presentation that can be termed *low-key Islam*; second, the active demonstration of capacities and skills associated with urban youth culture in the United States, or an emphasis on their *American abilities*; and finally, a rhetorical and demonstrated expression of the boys' autonomy and agency, especially in the arena of responses to discrimination, or *handling harassment*. Within their small group, and in interaction with the immediate social environment, the Legendz cultivated, refined, and combined these three tools for managing their public Muslim selves at a time of potential discrimination to form a relatively coherent method of self-presentation. Because these three practices and their underlying logic were so deeply rooted in the Legendz's small-group dynamics and processes, and because they so closely matched their immediate social environment, the boys' method of dealing with public Muslim selfhood possessed a structural integrity that made it a difficult match for the competing method promoted by City Mosque leaders.

PRESENTING A LOW-KEY ISLAMIC IDENTITY IN PUBLIC

The first of the boys' practices entailed presenting a low-key Islam in interaction with non-Muslims. Just as the Legendz in other areas of their lives sometimes symbolically deemphasized their obligatory rituals, eschewed overtly Islamic forms of popular culture, and participated in communally approved courtship protocol without explicitly labeling their actions "Islamic," so too they often made the Islamic dimension of their identity available but not central to their interactions with non-Muslims outside the community. In school, in their neighborhoods, and in other public spaces, the Legendz consistently told people that they were Muslim if the matter arose and answered questions about Islam if asked, but they did not actively assert an Islamic identity or allow this dimension of their American teenage selves to dominate their interactions with others, either symbolically or rhetorically. At hip hop performances at secular schools, at studio sessions with non-Muslim musicians, and at the boys' places of work, I found that people who worked alongside and made music with the boys knew that they were Muslim, and that the Legendz were willing to discuss and answer questions about Islam and the mosque when asked. At the same time, issues of Muslim identity or Islamic religiosity never dominated these situations. The Legendz were not hesitant or afraid to speak about their Muslim identity in public, but the internally incubated style of Muslim identity they extended into the public realm was recognizably one of *low-key Islam.*

Such a low-key presentation of Islamic identity is not the same as a consistent and intentional assertion of one's Muslim identity in public. The Legendz recognized and admitted the difference between their own orientation toward being Muslim in public and that of those who broadcast a more strongly and identifiably Islamic image through clothing, facial hair, or head coverings. When I asked Yusef about overt episodes of anti-Muslim harassment that he had experienced in school or other public settings, he could only remember one or two. When I pushed him to see if he could recall more, he said:

> YUSEF: I really can't remember, John, I'm sorry.
> JOHN: That's okay.
> YUSEF: Um, I don't know. We just get along with everybody . . . kind of thing. Like no—nobody has a problem with us, and we can relate to like almost anyone. Um, so for us, it's . . . I don't know, like . . . and we're really not, like, hardcore like Salafi [a very conservative form of Sunni Islam], like, or whatever . . . that our image is out there as Muslims.
> JOHN: Right.

YUSEF: So I guess we don't get discriminated like that . . . because of our image.

In this instance, Yusef associated the Legendz's understated Muslim public image ("not, like, hardcore") with the fact that they faced less harassment than did other, more visible, Muslims. Even though Yusef consistently told people at work and at school that he was Muslim, he distinguished this presentation from the more visible style of Muslim selfhood exemplified by a "Salafi," a person whose Muslim image was more "out there." Yusef and the other Legendz's identity as Muslims was well known to the non-Muslims in their regular circles, and they spoke openly about their religion in the company of these people. But their reluctance to visibly and actively assert their Muslim identity in public through dress, language, or more consistent and religious talk also probably helped shield them from more frequent and direct harassment, especially from strangers. When I asked Muhammad about his experiences with harassment, he said something similar to what Yusef had told me.

MUHAMMAD: Like myself, I . . . I don't . . . the thing . . . the thing . . . biggest thing about us, we look like normal kids . . . you know. I mean, if . . . if I went to school every day with a *thobe* [ankle-length garment] on [chuckles], you know, or a *kufi* [round cap], you know, some slippers, maybe for sure somebody would try to say something to me. You know . . . I'm . . . I've seen that happen. I know kids that, they go to school, like, came straight from, like, Saudi Arabia or whatever, and they . . . dress . . . like they did back home. . . . And I know for a fact they get made fun of, and they get tormented for . . . like, they might not understand it fully. . . . But they do, they go through it. And it might hurt them. But myself, I . . . we look like normal kids. And only—the only time it ever happens is when people hear my name or . . . or when I talk about it.

JOHN: Right.

MUHAMMAD: Because I'm not scared to tell people that I'm Muslim.

Here we can see the logic of a low-key public presentation of Muslim self at work. Muhammad stressed the fact that he and the other Legendz did not assert their Islamic identity by dressing in recognizably "Muslim" ways. At the same time—and my experiences observing him in non-Muslim spaces corroborated this—he said that he would sometimes "talk about" Islam at school, and that he was "not scared to tell people" that he was Muslim if the subject came up. Therefore, while the Legendz's Islamic identification was not usually dominant or central in their encounters with non-Muslims in public space, it was still present and available. The same low-key approach to the symbolic decentering of Islam that helped the Legendz feel like American teenagers among themselves as they tried to date, pray, and listen to music extended to the public sphere, where it provided them with a means of acknowledging their Muslim identity without drawing significant and possibly problematic attention to it.

As American teenagers, the Legendz were certainly not unique in seeking to strategically downplay their "inherited" identities in the public realm in order to win social acceptance. Young people, including working-class white and Latino teenagers and young African Americans from poor neighborhoods, often fear that their primary home-linked identities may clash with the dominant "prep," achievement-oriented, and European-centric culture of their public schools. As a result, they frequently make strategic adjustments to their self-presentations within their school context to fall more in line with the reigning cultural milieu.[2] This dilemma has been found to be particularly acute for immigrant youth from countries such as Mexico, Vietnam, or India, who often wish to fit into the broader social context of their school but also feel a desire and/or responsibility to maintain meaningful and visible connections with their families and ethnic communities.[3] For these young people, presenting a low-key ethnic or class identity at school—through subtle modifications to hair, clothing, or makeup or strategic alterations to their linguistic style or language spoken—provides a practical if imperfect solution for sustaining a degree of home-linked cultural identity in public while denying such a self-definition absolute prominence or symbolic centrality.

PUBLICLY DEMONSTRATING URBAN
AMERICAN TEENAGE CAPABILITIES

Although the Legendz's extension of their low-key presentation of Islamic selves into the public sphere appeared to have helped them avoid severe, ongoing harassment, the identification of the boys as Muslims due to their "different" names or discussion of their religion did occasionally trigger incidents of verbal or physical harassment by other youth. Whenever such incidents occurred, the Legendz found the demonstration of mastery over a locally valued and American teenage-associated skill or ability a consistently effective means of responding. Thus, the second core practice adopted by the boys in presenting themselves as Muslims in public involved their prioritization of identifiably "American teenage" capabilities and competencies over overtly "Islamic" practices and behaviors. Just as mastery over hip hop music or dating practices served as a means of demonstrating to each other that they were acceptably "American" teenagers in their in-group setting, so too did demonstrating skills in basketball, skateboarding, verbal comebacks, and physical fighting serve as practical means of displaying "normal" Americanness in direct response to potentially differentiating harassment. When I asked Tariq to tell me about any harassment he had suffered in school on account of his being Muslim, he replied:

> TARIQ: I would say the first time it happened was third grade. I went to a new elementary school, and they . . . because my full name is Tariq Abdullah Hamdani. So they're . . . they're like, when the teacher called out my name, they're like, "Oh, where you from?" Stuff like that. Then from there, they started, "Oh, you terrorist." Stuff like that.
> JOHN: Right.
> TARIQ: That happened. And around . . . I think around that time was the same time when, ah, 9/11 happened.
> JOHN: Okay.
> TARIQ: So from there it was just like . . . everyone that knew me. . . . Even, I had close friends that just like shunned me

out . . . for no reason, because, oh, I guess the popular kids were like, "Oh, this guy's Muslim, he probably has bombs in his backpack," or some shit like that.

Tariq went on to tell me how he and another Muslim student, Saif, had been repeatedly bothered by the same group of "popular kids." When I asked him how he had responded in such situations, he said:

TARIQ: To be honest with you, we just played basketball. That's, like, our little getaway.

JOHN: Right. Right.

TARIQ: We just used to play basketball. And when we played basketball, that was . . . I don't want to brag, because I used to be pretty good. . . . So I should take advantage of that . . . for all the people that used to talk, like, crap around me, I'm like, alright, cool, let's play basketball. And fuck, a little basketball, that's the reason why I love basketball, because when you play basketball you forget about everything.

JOHN: Yeah.

TARIQ: It's about who's going to win, who's better. . . . So that used to really, like . . . that was one way I used to get out of it.

JOHN: Yeah.

TARIQ: Just play basketball.

For Tariq, playing basketball was an effective response to anti-Muslim harassment not only because the activity took his mind off of the discrimination he faced, but also because it felt like a locally valued skill for which he could be assessed on his own individual merits rather than stigmatized on account of his cultural difference. Salman, an avid skateboarder who often experienced anti-Muslim and anti–South Asian slurs during citywide skateboarding competitions, spoke about the importance of skateboarding as a social equalizer in a strikingly similar way:

SALMAN: And for me, I think skateboarding was the biggest way I was able to cha—you know, to channel out Islam and be proud of it. Because one thing that skateboarding taught me was that, nowadays . . . how can you classify a skateboarder? Like when you stereotype a basketball player, you're probably thinking tall . . . black . . . you know. You know, or a soccer player . . . like, you know what I mean?

JOHN: Yeah.

SALMAN: But a skateboarder, you can't really stereotype skateboarders anymore. You know? Because skateboarding is such a sport where it's really based off of individualism, you know.

If Tariq and Salman responded to experiences of anti-Muslim discrimination by demonstrating their prowess in the locally recognized American teenage skills of basketball and skateboarding, the other Legendz discovered the power of a different ability valued within their public school environment: aggressive self-defense. By standing up for themselves either with words or with fists, Muhammad, Abdul, and Yusef demonstrated their capacity in a highly valued skill within their urban public school milieu and found that this strategy not only worked to stop their harassers but also won them a measure of recognition and credibility among their wider non-Muslim peer group. When I asked Yusef whether he had experienced much anti-Muslim harassment at school, he said:

YUSEF: No, no. Just, there's, like . . . honestly, in high school there was, ah . . . maybe in my ninth grade, like my freshman year there, there was like this fucking asshole . . . and his two friends that wouldn't stop bothering me, you know, for like the whole semester. . . . And . . . but, you know, my professor [sic] really didn't care. And it was, like, in class too, but my professor didn't care.

JOHN: Oh, wow.

YUSEF: My teacher didn't care.

JOHN: What kind of stuff would they say?

YUSEF: [laughs] Oh, my God. They would sing this song. It was just stupid. It was, ah . . . how did it go? Ah . . . okay, you know Red Man and Method Man?

JOHN: Yeah.

YUSEF: Yeah. They're like, "Zim Zimma, who's got the keys to my Beemer?" You know that song?

JOHN: Yeah, yeah.

YUSEF: Yeah? So they'd be like, they'd sing, "Osama, who's got the keys to my Humma?"

JOHN: Oh, gosh [laughs].

YUSEF: It's just . . . they'd be doing shit like that. And then they'd be, like, ah . . . they'd call me Osama, you know. They'd go, "Osama, what's up, man?" You know, like, blah-blah, just talking shit like that . . . just saying random things like, you know, ah, "You know who you gonna blow up next?" or "Who you gonna kill next?"—shit like that, you know. . . . Just kind of, like, try to get . . . try to get under my skin. And I would respond with, you know, just kind of like racial slurs about Hispanics and Mexicans [laughs].

JOHN: Yeah.

YUSEF: I would do that. And then like 90 percent of the classroom population was Hispanic [laughs]. . . . I wasn't the popular kid in that class [laughs] . . . but [laughs] . . .

JOHN: So what would happen after that?

YUSEF: Nothing. We just . . . we just went back and forth, and, um, one day we . . . it got a little physical. And, like, he ended up hitting me, then I ended up hitting him back. And it just kind of . . . that was it. Like he stopped after that.

JOHN: It was in class?

YUSEF: Yeah. During class. The teacher didn't do anything; he didn't say anything.

JOHN: Yeah.

YUSEF: He saw everything, he heard everything, and he knew what was going on for a really long time, but never said anything . . . but, yeah. So he hit me, then I hit him back, and then it just stopped.

Although Yusef had been experiencing ongoing verbal harassment from these students for a period of about three months, one physical response seems to have been sufficient to bring an end to this behavior and the hassle of having to deal with it. When I asked Yusef whether he thought that fighting back in this way had contributed to the end of the harassment, he said:

> YUSEF: Yeah. Because I guess they finally knew, like, okay, like, this boy, he, like, if he's going to get annoyed with us, he's going to actually hit us now. So I don't want to get hurt, so I'm going to stop talking shit, you know.
>
> JOHN: Yeah.
>
> YUSEF: I guess people always want the approval of others. So that's why, like, they're always talking shit in front of a lot of people, so that the people can be on their side. But, like, once they get hit, they feel a little embarrassed and they don't have that approval anymore, and they're like, okay, got to regain that somehow. . . . And they're not, like . . . I guess they . . . they stop talking shit, so they want to gain your approval, because you . . . you've gotten the respect of the class now that you've hit them, you know. So then they want to try to be friends with you, and, like, oh, have to redeem themselves, you know.

Yusef's account of the fight and its aftermath not only emphasized the effectiveness of fighting back but also revealed how the broader outcome of ending the harassment was related to his public *demonstration* of physical aggression. According to Yusef, his demonstration of physical force not only had shown the harasser that he could fight ("he's actually going to hit us now") but had also gained "the respect of the class." By displaying ability in a locally valued skill, Yusef moved himself from a status of social marginalization based on difference ("Osama," "Who you gonna blow up?") to one of social recognition ("respect," "they want to try to be friends").

In responding to harassment with aggression, Abdul and Muhammad took a less physical and more verbal approach, gaining recognition through their harsh and cutting insults. Abdul told me a story about how he had used verbal comebacks to put other kids in their place and to ease the harassment he faced:

ABDUL: So I would always come back with jokes. Like, there was this one time this kid—I forgot what he was saying—he's like, oh, you're . . . you're a terrorist, this and that. And I was like . . . I was like, yeah, well, that's because I terrorized your mom's pussy last night. Like, I would say stupid stuff like that . . .

JOHN: Right.

ABDUL: You know what I mean?

JOHN: Yeah.

ABDUL: And this other kid came back with braces, and he was talking . . . I forgot what he said to me, but I was like, "You really miss the border that much that you put, you know, a fence in your teeth?" . . . And he was like . . . and, like, he . . . it went around the whole school, and, like, the kid almost cried, you know, and I felt bad. But don't talk if you don't want . . . you know what I mean? If you're trying to roast me, I'll get back at you, you know. That's just how it was with me, you know. . . . That kid was so mad.

JOHN: Yeah. So what did he do?

ABDUL: Even his own . . . his own people were laughing at him, like everybody was laughing at him. And they laughed at it for about a week, which is kind of sad again, but . . .

JOHN: Right.

ABDUL: If you can't, you know, don't add fuel to a fire.

By translating anger at anti-Muslim comments into a locally recognizable language of mean and cutting insults or physical fights instead of, for example, asserting the virtues of their Islamic identity, the Legendz worked to defend their Muslimness in a way that simultaneously asserted their own urban American teenage cultural credentials and refused to deny or hide their Muslim identity. The social benefits of this kind of recognition can be seen here in Abdul's remark (which he uttered with audible pride) that the other kid's "own people were laughing at him, like, everybody was laughing at him. And they laughed for about a week." In this way, snappy verbal comebacks and physical fights served the boys as a means of not only pushing back against their harassers but also asserting their own extra-Islamic, American teenage normality by exploiting a locally meaningful skill to gain social recognition.

Demonstrating interest in or aptitude at particular activities is a well-established means by which young people in America appeal for access to particular and bounded social crowds, whether they turn to tricked-out cars to get in with the "low-riders," an aggressive fashion style to feel comfortable among "goths," or demonstrations of athletic prowess to be accepted as "jocks."[4] For culturally marginal outsiders such as young people from highly religious communities and immigrant youth, participation in locally valued activities in school often serves a more fundamental purpose: to act as an appeal for a general acceptance among peers and establish oneself as less fundamentally "strange" and more of a "normal" American teenager. Such strategic attempts have been observed among young evangelical Christians who brag about playing in rock bands, young Latinas who gain a reputation for excelling at basketball, and young people of various and diverse backgrounds who embrace hip hop culture.[5] I would argue that at this point in history, demonstrating verbal and physical aggression can also be considered a central expectation of mainstream American male youth culture and should therefore also be seen as a locally valued "activity" through which culturally marginal youth can attempt to work their way into a more socially accepted and more "American" position within their school and neighborhood cultural context.[6]

EMPHASIZING AGENCY AND AUTONOMY WHILE MANAGING HARASSMENT

The third core practice used by the Legendz to present themselves as Muslims in public involved emphasizing their ability to handle anti-Muslim discrimination and harassment on their own, that is, without the help or guidance of adults at the mosque or anyone else. Just as the Legendz applied individualistic discourses of autonomy and agency to Islamic ritual within the mosque, so too did they speak about dealing with and responding to anti-Muslim stigma and harassment in ways that stressed their own individual abilities to handle such challenges. Yusef expressed this sense of personal mastery over his responses to harassment one afternoon as I ate lunch with him and youth group leader Melvin at a Chinese restaurant across the street from the mosque. Over pan-fried noodles and dumplings, we discussed upcoming changes in the youth program and how Melvin was about to assume a more direct role in overseeing the group. I took this opportunity to ask what Yusef and Melvin thought of the facilitated discussions and skits regularly led by Omar in which he advised youth to respond to harassment by maintaining a peaceful demeanor and trying to represent Islam in a positive light.

> I ask Melvin, "So you're going to be running all the sessions?" He says, "Yeah." I say, "Because, you know those skits Omar would do, where it was like, 'What do you do if someone calls you names?' Do you guys think those are helpful?" There's a pause. "It depends who you are," Melvin says. Yusef nods. "Yeah, some people just don't know how to defend themselves."

Yusef's answer implied that the exercises aimed at teaching young Muslims in the mosque how to respond to harassment were useless to *him*, because he already knew how to defend himself. He did, however, admit that there might have been some other kids who didn't know how to defend themselves from anti-Muslim harassment and therefore needed the help or guidance of adults, but he made it clear that he did not belong in this category.

Muhammad expressed a similar swaggering confidence about the Legendz's ability to handle and shut down incidents of harassment on their own. Following up on a finding that initially puzzled me, I asked Muhammad directly why he thought that the Legendz spoke and thought about anti-Muslim discrimination and harassment so rarely.

> JOHN: Because it's funny, when I talk to people about this
>   book, people are surprised that you guys aren't . . . talking
>   about that more, that you guys . . . aren't dealing with
>   that more. Because so much of your life is about music,
>   or friends, or other stuff . . . people are almost surprised

> that that [harassment] is not happening all the time or
> something, you know?
> MUHAMMAD: I mean, the reason why is because . . . because
> we don't let it happen.

In an answer that dramatically stripped away all social factors as potential explanations for why the Legendz did not discuss anti-Muslim discrimination more often, Muhammad rhetorically boiled the reason down to the Legendz's autonomous action and individual ability to defend themselves. This belief—that they were fully capable of defending themselves against harassment—was attractive to the boys for the same reason that it appeals to diverse constituencies of urban American teenagers, and especially young men of color[7]: it demonstrates both a broadly desirable American individualism and a locally significant, masculine, urban American "cool."

The City Mosque Method for Being a Young Muslim in Public

As we have seen, the Legendz's method for managing their public Muslim identity within a potentially stigmatizing climate centered on three core practices: their presentation of a low-key Islamic self, their demonstration of American teenage capacities, and their insistence that they could handle harassment and discrimination themselves. However, at the same time that the Legendz were cultivating and implementing this method, City Mosque leaders were working to promote their own alternative set of strategies for managing Muslim youth identity in the post-9/11 era. According to the logic of mosque leadership—logic transmitted to youth members through workshops, trainings, and interfaith meetings—there were three preferred strategies for dealing with this problem. First, young Muslims should fully and actively present their Muslim identity to others and explain Islam to non-Muslims. In other words, they should engage in what I call *leading with Islam*. Second, when interacting with non-Muslims, young Muslims should be willing and able to display a *noble vulnerability*, especially regarding the anti-Muslim harassment they faced. Finally, young Muslims should concern themselves with the image of Islam among non-Muslims and engage in *appeals to non-Muslims* for sympathy and understanding. While these three practices were consistently promoted by mosque leaders through youth program meetings, interfaith visits, and other activities, they also met with regular resistance from the Legendz, whose internally cultivated and maintained method of stigma management and presentation of public Muslim selfhood often stood in direct conflict with the method endorsed by the mosque leadership.

LEADING WITH ISLAM IN A CLIMATE OF SUSPICION

City Mosque leadership—especially Omar and youth group volunteer Michael—consistently reminded the youth at the mosque that they should readily present themselves *as Muslims* in public and explain their religion to others. Mosque adults articulated the general principle that young Muslims should be proud of their identity and explain their religion to others during youth program meetings, classes, and talks. But this emphasis on identifying oneself as Muslim and explaining Islam was connected to mosque leaders' belief that young Muslims had a particularly pressing responsibility to present a positive and reassuring image of Muslims and Islam in the post-9/11 climate of suspicion and stereotyping. So, while the Legendz were used to presenting themselves in public in a way that downplayed their Muslim identity and maintained a low-key identification with the religion, mosque leaders encouraged Muslim youth to *lead with* Islam, to actively present it, explain it, and try to clear up any misconceptions held by non-Muslims about it and its adherents.

About six months into my time at the City Mosque, Shazia, a young woman who had been the leader of the youth group for many years, announced that she would be leaving the mosque because she was moving to Egypt. This news was quite upsetting to the Legendz, who had grown up at the mosque under her tutelage. One of the consequences of her announcement was an intensive rethinking of how the youth program would now be run. Long brainstorming sessions were held with youth group leaders Michael, Melvin, and

Shazia and other veteran youth group members such as the Legendz, Nailah, and Sana. During one such session, the discussion narrowed down to the question of criteria for youth program membership, and Michael asked rhetorically:

> What kind of requirements should we have for being in the youth group? Well, number one could be knowing what a Muslim is. You have to know the fundamentals of being a Muslim. If not, you're just here hanging out. I want you to be able to go to your school and tell them who you are and how you pray and what Ramadan is. And not be afraid to say who you are.

For Michael, the most significant requirement of membership in the youth program was that members should "know the fundamentals of being a Muslim." This sounds reasonable enough, but what is notable is how quickly this turned into going "to your school" to "tell *them* who you are and how you pray and what Ramadan is" (italics mine). While such an entreaty might just as easily be heard within any other religious group seeking to expand its outreach in the community, Michael's insistence that the youth "not be afraid" linked his advice to concerns about potential anti-Muslim stigma. Time and again within the mosque setting, conversations ostensibly about fostering young Muslims' religious or cultural practices within and for themselves turned seamlessly into exhortations to Muslim teenagers to represent and explain Islam to others in public, and to do so out of a sense of moral responsibility.

The same appeal to Muslim youth to represent Islam in public arose during a youth group conversation led by a guest speaker named Khaled. Initially this talk was directed at encouraging young Muslims to carry out their obligatory five daily prayers. As the conversation continued, however, some youth in attendance admitted that sometimes they did not pray, especially in public places, because they were embarrassed by the possibility of someone seeing them.

> At this point, Michael says, with some exasperation, "OK, but I think it's important for us to talk about why everyone is afraid to let someone else see them pray." One girl says, "Because it's

something different." "That's right," Khaled says. "It's something different, and it's not something that people are used to. Why else are we afraid to let people see us pray?" Musa says, "Because people start asking you questions, and then you have to answer everything for them." Michael interjects to say, "But I see that as a good thing, because then I have the chance to teach someone about Islam."

Once again, Michael turned a conversation about fulfilling religious obligations into an appeal for Muslim youth to actively represent Islam in public. This message—that representing and explaining Islam to others is part and parcel of being a modern American Muslim young person—was reinforced by Khaled once again during the same session. Just before the meeting came to an end, Khaled advised the group not to be afraid to pray in public or to explain Islamic rituals to others, saying, "I think if we open up, people will understand us better. People are curious, they just don't know. But people need to get used to the fact that there are 6 to 10 million [*sic*] Muslims in the US."

Although "opening up" and explaining Islam to non-Muslims was consistently emphasized by mosque leaders, it was not a priority shared either by most youth at the mosque or by the Legendz. While the Legendz generally informed people about Islamic practices and traditions when asked, they were equally likely to overtly shirk and resist this kind of "ambassadorial" work, especially when it felt as though they were being pressured into it. The mosque leaders' expectation that youth represent and answer for Islam in public thus stood in tension with the Legendz's emphasis on personal autonomy in the presentation of their Muslim selves.

The Legendz and other Muslim youth often characterized answering questions about Islam as a chore and something that they felt put upon to do. Muhammad elucidated this perspective to me during a car ride one late afternoon in the month of Ramadan. We had been fasting all day and were driving to the suburban home of Bilal, another youth group member, whose family was holding an *iftar*, a fast-breaking dinner, that evening. As I drove, Muhammad sat in the passenger seat, holding a closed tin of brownies in his lap. At one point, I asked him how fasting was going at school. This led to a conversation about other Muslim kids at his school:

> "And there are a few other Muslim kids at your school, right?" I ask. "Yeah," he says. "There's one kid from Nigeria, but he's not fasting. And that other kid Ibrahim, he is fasting. . . . I think there are other Muslim kids in our school, but they're hiding. They don't want to come out as Muslim." "Huh. . . . You and your brothers were never like that, right?" I ask. "No," he says, shaking his head. "I always tell people I'm Muslim." "Why do you think the kids who don't tell people . . . why do you think they do that?" He says, "I think it's because they don't want to answer so many questions about being Muslim. Like, whenever I tell someone I'm Muslim, they ask me a whole bunch of questions about the religion and why we do what we do. And sometimes I don't even know the answer, and I'm like, 'You know, I don't know that.'"

Although Muhammad presented himself in this conversation as someone generally willing to answer questions about Islam—which, in my experience, he was—his description of Muslim students "hiding" at school as well as his own account of being asked "a whole bunch of questions" illustrated a sentiment that I heard from each of the Legendz as well as from other youth at the mosque: that answering questions about Islam from non-Muslims frequently felt like a frustrating burden. This sentiment was also evident in a comment Yusef made during a youth group session one Sunday morning. As will be discussed further later, this particular meeting was attended by a liberal reverend named James Francis, who wished to learn about the experiences of young Muslims and who expressed support for the mosque community in times of anti-Muslim bias. During the discussion, the reverend asked whether any of the youth could share a story or experience of being a Muslim teenager. Omar volunteered Yusef to speak. Looking straight at Reverend Francis, Yusef said in a serious tone, "All the time you have to make everybody understand. . . . You have to respect yourself. You have to explain to people about Islam and that we don't worship Muhammad." His weighty tone and use of "have to" suggest that this job of explaining and answering questions about Islam was something that he experienced not as a slightly annoying responsibility—which is how mosque adults often characterized it—but as an exhausting and frustrating task that felt coercive rather than voluntary.

The practice of leading with Islam in public was undesirable to the Legendz not only because it threatened their sense of autonomy, but also because it conflicted with their preferred low-key mode of Islamic identity and was often seen as playing into associations between Islam and stereotypes about terrorism and violence. When asked to represent Islam in this way, the Legendz sometimes overtly resisted. I witnessed an example of this kind of resistance one afternoon at the mosque as I stood in the main lobby with Abdul and Drew, a non-Muslim friend who had accompanied him to the mosque that day. On this particular afternoon, we were selling candy bars to raise funds for the youth program.

Abdul, Drew, and I stand behind the table, making ourselves available to sell candy to passersby. I notice a group of three college-aged people who I don't recognize walk in the front door of the mosque—two women and a man, and two of them are carrying notebooks. I watch as they walk up to the front desk and say something to Thomas, who is stationed there as usual. After listening to them for a few minutes, Thomas waves for mosque volunteer Aimen, who is nearby, and Abdul to come over and speak to them. Aimen obediently walks over to the group of three and begins talking with them. I can't figure out if they are here for an event or something. Abdul does not move but turns his head slightly towards me and says, kind of under his breath, "I don't want to go talk to them." Nonetheless, he does walk slowly in that general direction, but ends up standing to the right of Aimen, so he's in the vicinity but not actually speaking to the three visitors at all. As Aimen starts to walk with the group towards the prayer area, Abdul peels off and circles back towards the candy table. "I don't want to talk to those people," he says to me again as he arrives back near Drew and me. "Who are they?" I ask him. "I don't know," he says. "They want to learn about the mosque or something." "Oh, they're students or something?" I ask. "Yeah," he says. "They probably have an assignment to learn about the mosque. . . . I don't like doing that." "Why don't you like doing it?" I ask him. He's leaning back against the wall between the bookstore and the community room, with his arms tucked behind his back. "Because they ask too many questions. I don't like answering all of their questions." "Why don't you like answering their questions?" I ask him. "I don't know," he says. "I don't know the answers to most of the questions they ask me." We stand there behind the candy table. I look over and see Aimen talking to the group of three, gesturing with his arms towards the prayer area. "Why do you think people like that come here so much?" I ask Abdul. He says, "Because they want to know about Muslims, and understand us." "Why do you think they want to know about us?" I ask him. He looks down and kind of mutters, "Because we're the world's biggest terrorists, supposedly." "You think that's why they want to understand us?" I ask. "Yeah," he says. "We're in the news all the time."

Here we can see two different strands of resistance to the mosque leadership's consistent expectation that young Muslims be ready and willing to explain Islam and Muslims to non-Muslims at a moment's notice. Like Muhammad and the other youth discussed earlier, Abdul expressed his dislike for answering non-Muslims' questions about Islam. Illustrating how the pressure of this expectation pulled against his insistence on autonomy, Abdul first grudgingly acknowledged that he was expected to stop and talk to these visitors but then resisted, altering the response that was clearly expected and desired by Thomas. A second issue behind this resistance is also equally evident here: the perception that a quick and ready response to non-Muslims' inquiries about Islam serves to place Islam, and likely specific popular and negative associations with Islam, front and center in the interaction. Abdul strongly resisted this encounter with the visitors in part because he anticipated that the questions these people would ask him about "Muslims" would almost inevitably be linked to stereotypes about "terrorists." Such encounters thus struck Abdul and the other Legendz as conflicting with their autonomous presentation of a low-key Islam. Predicting that any interaction with the non-Muslim visitors would be centered on Islam in a narrow way that would be essentially out of his control, Abdul strongly resisted it.

DEMONSTRATING A NOBLE VULNERABILITY TO ISLAMOPHOBIA

If one tenet of the mosque leadership's preferred model for presenting a public young Muslim self in a climate of potential stigma centered on being ready and willing to explain Islam to non-Muslims, a second encouraged young Muslims to present themselves as noble subjects who were regularly vulnerable to anti-Muslim discrimination. Through the production of media about Muslim youth, facilitated meetings with non-Muslim visitors to the mosque, and direct advice to young Muslim members, mosque leaders encouraged youth to share their experiences as subjects of anti-Muslim discrimination. While this public image of Muslim youth was certainly not the only one that the mosque leaders wished to promote, the notion that mosque youth should present themselves as vulnerable to harassment and discrimination was a consistent focus of mosque leaders' activities. As with their attempt to promote public explanations of Islam, however, this plea directly conflicted with core elements of the Legendz's method of presenting a Muslim identity in public, and especially with their insistence on defining themselves by their abilities and autonomy, including their ability to handle harassment on their own. Although mosque leaders consistently worked to promote the view that Muslim youth were vulnerable to harassment and discrimination, their attempts to do so were regularly resisted by the Legendz, in ways both subtle and overt.

The interfaith visit was one type of gathering at which youth at the mosque were regularly encouraged to present themselves as subjects of anti-Muslim harassment. On these occasions, which were nominally concerned with sharing information between members of different religions, both mosque leaders and non-Muslim visitors encouraged Muslim youth to open up and talk about their daily lives. These conversations almost invariably became dominated by the theme of anti-Muslim harassment. The sharing of personal harassment stories by youth provided an opportunity for mosque leaders, in collaboration with sympathetic non-Muslim adult and youth visitors, to portray and understand Muslim youth as emotionally vulnerable subjects who deserved sympathy and acceptance. One example of this phenomenon took place on a Sunday morning when the liberal Reverend Francis, mentioned earlier, came to visit the youth group. After a brief introduction by Omar, who reminded the group of the reverend's extensive activism on behalf of American Muslims and against the war in Iraq, the priest looked out at the assembled group of about twenty-five young people and said:

> "I've been thinking about what it must be like to be a teenager in the US right now, to be teenagers who are Muslim." Yusef looks at the reverend. "My teen years are when my ethics came together. I would like to know something about you before I say anything else. What is it like to be a teenager in this city who is Muslim? What is that like on a day-to-day basis? Maybe you can give me a story or a description." There's a pause as he waits for someone to respond. It doesn't feel like an unnaturally long pause, but religious director Omar quickly jumps in and says, "I might have to volunteer some people. . . . Yusef?"

Yusef's story, referenced earlier, initially dealt with his frustration at answering questions about Islam but then moved on to recount more overt incidents of harassment:

> "Sometimes they will call you a terrorist. Sometimes I don't mind that because it's ignorance. I know what I believe, so I don't even trip [worry]. I just ignore it because I know it isn't true. . . . It's not even funny, though, sometimes. It's like 'whoa' [pushes his hands down in the air with the palms down]." The reverend asks, "You feel a lot of anger?" Yusef says, "Yes."

In what was a typical scene during such a visit, Omar encouraged young Muslims to speak about their daily lives to non-Muslim outsiders. Although the reverend's question did not explicitly refer to harassment or Islamophobia, the vast majority (seven out of nine) of the stories told by the attending youth in response to his request that day dealt directly with experiences of anti-Muslim harassment and discrimination. As Yusef and the other youth recounted these stories, Omar and the reverend looked on and nodded sympathetically, sometimes offering comments that validated the young people's feelings of frustration and anger. The reverend told the youth it was good for them to speak and think about these experiences instead of fighting back, because such a response would show that they were superior to the "little-minded" and "petty" people who harassed them.

A scene from another interfaith visit to the youth group—this time by members of a Jewish youth group and their rabbi—further illustrates the ongoing attempts of mosque leaders and outside visitors to cast Muslim youth as vulnerable subjects of discrimination. In this particular instance, the cultural friction between the Legendz's commitment to demonstrating their capability and autonomy and the mosque adults' cultivation of vulnerability and sympathy became visible in an exchange between Omar and Yusef. After the group of about twelve Jewish students arrived and everyone had settled into their seats and been introduced to each other, the rabbi spoke:

"Now we want to give you guys a chance to talk to each other, and we wanted to start by giving the group from my temple a chance to ask questions they have about Islam. Does that sound OK?" Everybody nods yes. "So who would like to start? We spent a little time thinking of questions before we came, so we should have some. . . ."A girl sitting to my right raises her hand. "Hi. My name is Carla. There's been a lot of discrimination against Muslims and Islam lately. Have any of you experienced that? Because of stereotypes that are floating around?" There is silence as no one initially volunteers to speak. Omar says, "Anybody want to share their experiences?"

Yusef says, "I've experienced a lot, in middle school and in elementary school. People would call me terrorist. . . . I got mad, and I was about to get into a fight. The teacher broke up the fight. But the teacher didn't even care. She didn't tell him to stop. The same boy was talking about me again. . . . So I made fun of his mom." People in the group laugh at this. "That made him real mad."

Omar kind of rolls his eyes at this and says, "So the question is: How do you respond? . . . The Qur'an says, 'Respond to what is evil with what is good and the one who is your worst enemy will become your good friend.'" A boy with braids nods. "If someone says you are a violent person and you punch them, that's not a good response, right? . . . Sorry to pick on you, Yusef." Yusef smiles with his head down.

Here again, an interfaith visit became an occasion for visitors and mosque leaders to encourage youth to speak about themselves as subjects of anti-Muslim harassment and discrimination. While Omar seemed to expect, and possibly hope, that Yusef's story (like so many others) would serve to illustrate a sympathetic and morally upstanding young Muslim's vulnerability to harassment in public, Yusef's self-presentation was shaped by a different set of cultural concerns, foremost his desire to demonstrate his ability to respond to harassment on his own by utilizing the locally valuable social skill of assertive verbal response ("So I made fun of his mom"). While the Jewish kids laughed in a way that may have signaled their own positive valuation of Yusef's verbal comeback, any possibility of mutual understanding on this basis was left unexplored. Instead, Omar stepped in to repair the interaction by bringing Yusef's presentation of a capable, autonomous Muslim self more in line with the mosque's preferred depiction of a young Muslim facing discrimination as a vulnerable and conciliatory subject of harassment.

With the exception of Yusef's account of his verbal comeback, the Legendz generally went along with the attempts of mosque leaders and visitors to portray them as sympathetic subjects of harassment while in their presence. In side conversations and away from the mosque, however, they often expressed frustration at being presented to others in this way. Muhammad, for example, complained to me about his depiction in a video on Islamophobia that had been filmed at the mosque. I first heard about this video on the day it was filmed, a Sunday morning during my first few months at the mosque, after Sara, an employee with the mosque's affiliated nonprofit advocacy group, unexpectedly walked into a youth group meeting:

> Just as we are about to begin a new activity, Sara walks in the door. She's wearing a blue hijab and long-sleeved white shirt. She says, "Hello everyone! I need a few moments of your time. Last time, people shared their experiences with hate crimes and Islamophobia. Have any of you experienced this kind of thing?" Many people raise their hands, about twenty-five or so. "I want to see if any of you can be part of an interview we're going to do downstairs right now. It won't be high pressure, just a chill conversation. If you're down to be part of it, let me know, because we need volunteers right away."

What followed was an impromptu video shoot on the bleachers behind the mosque led by Sara and her video assistant, Asif. In the course of this session, twelve different stories about anti-Muslim harassment were shared by eight youth from the mosque, including Yusef and Muhammad. While the stories emphasized each subject's specific experiences of harassment and response, the framing of the discussion emphasized the position of Muslim youth as subjects of discrimination and harassment buffeted by the broad social forces of "Islamophobia" and "stereotyping." As she prepared the kids gathered on the bleachers to be videotaped, Sara introduced the topic of "Islamophobia" once again, informing them, "We're trying to raise people's awareness of it and start to understand it and then do something about it." During the video shoot, Muhammad described an incident experienced by his brother at school:

> They called my older brother "Saddam" because his middle name is Hussein, and they don't understand it. He hit me in my face. I hit him back. He started fighting with me and saying things like,

"Terrorist, I'm gonna get you after school." In class my teacher was talking about Muslims and said, "They do believe that blowing up people is all right."

Just as Yusef had told his story to the Jewish group, so too did Muhammad recount his initial response to being harassed and hit as standing up for himself and physically fighting back. However, in a move similar to Omar's correction of Yusef's admission of verbally fighting back during the Jewish youth visit, Muhammad's account of fighting was edited out of the final version of the video. The story in the final version went as follows: "They called my older brother 'Saddam' because his middle name is Hussein, and they don't understand it. He hit me in my face. . . . In class my teacher was talking about Muslims and said, 'They do believe that blowing up people is alright.'" This portrayal of Muhammad as a vulnerable subject of harassment and discrimination may have been more suitable for the mosque leadership's preferred narrative about Muslim youth, but it made Muhammad angry.

In June of 2007, the youth group held a "graduation" event at the City Mosque during which youth group members graduating from either eighth or twelfth grade were honored by the mosque community. All of the Legendz attended the event, as did many members of the youth group, mosque staff, and parents. After the formal ceremony was over, I stood in the social hall at the back of the mosque chatting with Muhammad about the graduation.

> Muhammad says, "I'm just glad they didn't show that movie." "What movie?" I ask. "You know, that Islamophobia one," he says. I nod. "Oh yeah. I saw that." He says, "They made me look like a punk." "What do you mean?" I ask. "You know in the end, when I put my head down? They make it in slow motion so I look all sad. I look like a punk, man." "No you don't," I say. "You didn't look like a punk." "I don't like that movie," he says. "I'm glad they didn't show it."

What made Muhammad particularly annoyed was the fact that the movie portrayed him as someone who was weak in the face of discrimination and emphasized his vulnerability rather than his strength. To the frustration of Muhammad and the other Legendz, the mosque leadership consistently insisted on portraying Muslim youth as emotionally vulnerable victims of powerful processes of anti-Muslim discrimination instead of as capable youth who could aggressively defend themselves against harassment.

CENTRALIZING CONCERN WITH NON-MUSLIMS; APPEALING TO THEM FOR HELP

In addition to encouraging a readiness to explain Islam to others and emphasizing youth's vulnerability to harassment, the mosque-endorsed method of managing a young Muslim identity in public differed from that developed by the Legendz in a third important way: it urged Muslim youth to prioritize the perspectives of non-Muslims toward Muslims and to try to win their favorable opinion, even and especially in situations of potential or actual anti-Muslim stigmatization. In stories meant to exemplify the "appropriate" response to harassment and in lectures on the best strategy for gaining wider acceptance in America, mosque leaders continually stressed the importance of improving non-Muslims' opinion of Muslims. A discussion that took place one Friday evening at the mosque just before the youth program members and staff left for a weekend-long retreat exemplifies the way in which Omar and others prioritized changing the perceptions and concerns of non-Muslims as a crucial way of improving the social status of Muslims in America. After reading a few brief verses from the Qur'an on the importance of Muslims sharing their faith with others, the group conversation turned to the prevailing image of Muslims and Islam in the United States:

> Omar says, "The verse tells us to spread Islam by telling people about Islam and behaving like a good person. Our responsibility is to clarify what we believe to others and act based on these beliefs, but not to compel others. . . . One of the things we're going to do on the retreat is make a YouTube video called iPray, and we're going to think of creative ways to do it. So we need to

work with others and share our faith with them." One boy raises his hand and says, "But the image of Muslims isn't like that at all!" "Right," says Omar. "And what can we as Muslim people do about that?" The boy says, "Right now they see people that are crazy—bombs and war and all that stuff." Omar says, "Bombs and war and we're scary and foaming at the mouth. . . . Is this how we see ourselves?" People shake their heads no. "So how can we change that image?" Omar asks. One boy says, "We can change ourselves." Omar says, "OK, we can change ourselves, dig deeper into our faith. What else?" A man in his thirties says, "We can read the Qur'an?" Omar says, "OK, read the Qur'an and try to follow the example of the Prophet." One boy says, "Try to convince the angry people to stop." Omar says, "OK, that's a good idea." He calls on another man, who says, "Maybe a better line is to keep trying and never give up." A boy raises his hand, Omar calls on him, and he says, "How will the crazy people stop doing that?" "That's a good question," Omar says. "What can we do?" Khaled says, "One way is to lead by your example and not be one. We'll not get that image. They will come and actually meet us." Omar says, "Yes. When they meet someone who is a real person, not someone who changes their name from Muhammed to Mo." People laugh. "Or from Osama to Oz." People laugh. "Or from Maryam to Mary. . . . But when people know you're a Muslim and see that you're not crazy, what a difference that makes. When they think of Muslims, they'll think of you."

This conversation's focus shifted from dangerous other Muslims who might be stopped ("the angry people," "the crazy people") to the City Mosque Muslims and their ability to alter their behavior ("we can change ourselves") before ultimately settling on non-Muslim others whose opinions of Islam were perceived as needing to be changed. It was this final group and its perspective that received Omar's most energetic response, and this imagined audience of non-Muslims that loomed largest in his advice to the group: "When *they* meet someone," "when *people* know," "when *they* think of Muslims." Mosque youth were thus taught to consider non-Muslims' perceptions of them and how Muslims could change these perceptions as if these concerns were the most centrally crucial factors in improving the lot of American Muslims.

Omar and other mosque leaders encouraged youth to take the perceptions of non-Muslims into account when in public but stressed that it was especially important to do so during incidents of harassment or discrimination. Just as Omar had urged Yusef during the Jewish youth group visit to respond to harassment in a nonviolent way because this response might improve his harasser's perspective of him, mosque leaders taught youth that when faced with harassment, they should always think about and try to amend the perpetrator's perspective on Islam and Muslims. This same logic was on display during a visit to the youth program by a pair of conflict mediators, one of whom asked the group:

"Does anyone have an example of a conflict they have experienced at school, with a teacher or a friend, or a nonfriend? Any kind of misunderstanding?" There is a very brief pause. Omar says, "Come on, you guys. Has anyone had a problem with teachers about Islam? Something they just said offhand? Come on, you guys. I know we've talked about this. . . ." A boy who is fairly new to the group says, "Well . . . when I went to my new middle school . . . it was mixed religion, and I think . . . I think I was the only Muslim in the whole school. And some people looked at me like I was strange, and they were like, 'When he grows up, he's gonna be a terrorist. I can see it already.' When I walked down the hall, people would stare at me, look at me like, 'What's up with you?'" Omar says, "So, what did you do? How did you handle it?" He says, "Well, I told my advisor, who was, like, my teacher, and she felt bad for me. She got the person that messed with me, and she brought him into class and he apologized. He stopped doing it, and now he's one of my best friends." The guest speaker says, "See, so conflict can actually be used as an opportunity. And I really applaud your advisor for what she did." Omar shakes his head in wonder. "You know, we've talked about this verse in the Qur'an before, but there's a verse that says that you should respond to evil with goodness until the person who is your worst enemy will become your best friend. And that's what you did. You didn't call him names; you took it as an opportunity. You didn't have ill will towards him. You used it as an opportunity to open up and express your concerns."

Here again, the harassment of a Muslim youth was portrayed as an occasion to consider the perspective of the non-Muslim harasser toward Islam, an opportunity to reach out to non-Muslims, and a chance to forge a positive relationship based on mutual understanding with such individuals. Omar celebrated this story because it aligned with the general narrative of harassment and response favored by the mosque, namely, that if Muslim youth presented themselves as vulnerable subjects of discrimination to non-Muslim others, then these others would come to accept and befriend Muslim youth. In contrast to the method used by the Legendz, the approach recommended by the mosque presented non-Muslims and their perceptions of Islam, rather than the harassers' actions or Muslim self-sufficiency, as the central concern. By consistently prioritizing the needs and concerns of non-Muslims at moments of harassment, the mosque leadership repeatedly sent the message that non-Muslims were important people worthy of attention whose opinions and perceptions were crucial to improving the social standing of non-Muslims.

The mosque encouraged this perception of non-Muslims as central players in the process of reducing Muslim harassment, but such a focus stood in tension with two core tenets of the Legendz's method of managing a Muslim identity in public: first, their ability to handle harassment and discrimination on their own; and, second, their ability to do so in part by downplaying the relevance of Islam to any such incident. Not only did the Legendz want to demonstrate that they could handle these situations themselves, but they generally did so in ways that displayed their *extra*-Islamic abilities—skateboarding, basketball, verbal comebacks, physical fighting—rather than by engaging in the question of the contested public image of Islam and Muslims. While the mosque leaders' concern with non-Muslims' perception of Muslims led naturally to a desire to change this perception, the

Legendz were unwilling to enter into this debate and instead spoke and acted in ways that sometimes revealed an intentional rejection of the prioritization of the concerns of non-Muslims. One way in which they expressed a flippant disregard for the perceptions of non-Muslim audiences among themselves was by making jokes that intentionally and dramatically invoked views of Muslims as violent terrorists, an act that mosque leadership would certainly never have found acceptable. Such local, minor deviant acts allowed the Legendz to express their dissatisfaction with the mosque's constant concern with non-Muslim perceptions without openly challenging it. I witnessed an example of this locally deviant self-stereotyping one afternoon during the mosque's annual convention, an event that brought together an array of speakers and participants from across the country to consider the issues facing Muslims in America.

> After attending a poetry workshop with some of the Legendz, I walk with them into the main hall of the convention center, where a Muslim Youth Program table is positioned at a central location. The table is arranged with flyers, some candy to sell, and the brand new MYP T-shirts that feature Arabic script. Abdul sees the black T-shirt with the Arabic writing on the back and jokingly leans over it in an overly intensive manner, and puts on a "white" voice: "Um, what is this writing? Are you guys selling terrorist T-shirts over here?" He points to the Arabic script, the beginning of which is a series of vertical lines, and says, in his own voice, "It says 1–2–3–4. . . . It says, 'I bombed your building.'" Fuad overhears this and laughs really hard. Abdul continues the joke, turning to Ali: "Hey Ali, you know what this says?" Ali shrugs. Abdul says, "I bombed your building." Ali opens his mouth wide and throws his head back, looking a little shocked, and laughs heartily. Abdul tells a few more people his joke.

As should be clear by now, the Legendz and their friends were not people who endorsed terrorist attacks in the name of Islam or celebrated bombings by terrorist groups. The reason why the joke was funny in this context was because it radically deviated from the ever-present concern with the perception of Muslims by non-Muslims that was cultivated by the mosque leadership within the youth program. Youth program members like Fuad and Ali were the ideal audience for the joke because they had experienced consistent exhortations by mosque leaders to consider how they represented Islam to others, even and especially in the context of potential harassment. Abdul's joke provided a release for the youth, as it allowed them to enact in private the opposite of what was generally a consistent social expectation put upon them.

Muhammad openly articulated a rejection of the mosque's consistent concern with non-Muslim audiences when I asked him one day about his experiences with harassment, and he told me that when such incidents happened, he often responded to their perpetrators harshly. In his response, he referred to Dr. Mubarak, a senior leader of the mosque.

> MUHAMMAD: Because some people are like, "Oh, like, we
> need to show . . ." from what I've learned from the mosque,
> like, from Dr. Mubarak and everybody, they want you to be
> an American Muslim where you prove to them that you're
> an American, you're not just a Muslim, you're an American
> too. Patriotic pride, just show it like that. But you don't have
> to. I don't have to prove to you that I'm an American. I don't
> have to prove to you shit, I don't have to teach . . . tell you
> that I'm a peaceful person, you know, that my religion is
> peaceful. I don't have to teach you none of that.
>
> JOHN: Right.
>
> MUHAMMAD: You know? If you feel that much where you can
> come and disrespect who I am and what I believe in . . . then
> you best believe it when I tell you something back and make
> you feel the same way that you made me feel.

Muhammad thus pushed back against the mosque leadership's prioritization of non-Muslim audiences ("you prove to *them* that you're an American") by assertively rejecting this concern as something he was obligated to take on. While the mosque leadership viewed incidents of anti-Muslim harassment as opportunities to focus on the perceptions of non-Muslims about Islam, Muhammad and the

Legendz took the opposite approach, stressing that it was not the responsibility of young Muslims to improve non-Muslims' perceptions of them, especially during times of harassment.

Conclusion

This chapter has demonstrated how two competing methods for the presentation of Muslim identity at a time of potential stigma coexisted and sometimes conflicted at the City Mosque. Such internal cultural friction resulted from the fact that these methods for managing stigma were rooted in two distinct models of public Muslim selfhood, one developed by the Legendz through the in-group processes of their small friendship group, and one constructed by the mosque leadership as their ideal model for Muslim American youth. While the mosque leadership method of presenting young Muslim selves centered on leading with and explaining Islam, demonstrating vulnerability to harassment, and developing concern for non-Muslims' perceptions, the method cultivated by the Legendz prioritized the development of a low-key Islamic self, an emphasis on locally valued American teenage behaviors, and the expression of individual autonomy and self-sufficiency.

Although these two methods rarely provoked major, visible conflict at the mosque at first, as the Legendz spoke further with me about these issues over time, it became clear that these differing logics of public identity management represented a significant rift between the Legendz and the leadership and sometimes even undermined the boys' faith and trust in the mosque adults. This development was a surprising and emotionally intense experience for the Legendz, who for years regularly expressed their appreciation for the efforts and openness of these leaders when it came to other aspects of their young American Muslim lives such as hip hop music, romantic dating, and religious ritual. On the issue of the public presentation of the Muslim self at a time of potential harassment, however, the Legendz felt and expressed a significant sense of disappointment in the mosque. After my fieldwork had ended, I contacted Muhammad to ask him, among other things, his opinion on the consistent message relayed by the mosque leadership to the Legendz and other Muslim youth that they should respond to harassment by not fighting back because such a response gave non-Muslims a negative image of Islam. His anger was as direct as I'd ever heard it:

> JOHN: At the mosque, whenever you guys would talk about this, Omar would always say things like, "Don't get mad," you know, "Don't fight back if somebody at school does this."
> MUHAMMAD: Yeah.
> JOHN: You know.
> MUHAMMAD: Fuck Omar.
> JOHN: [laughs] So what do you think about that?
> MUHAMMAD: Eh . . . I mean, to me, that's BS. Because it's, like, it's not about fighting back. I mean . . . not fighting as far as physical fighting. Getting angry. Getting angry is different. Like, I mean, there's at no point you should let anybody, like, bully you, you know? Like, you should never, in life, in whatever you do. . . . Don't let nobody talk down to you, talk like . . . Like, stand up for yourself.

While the method for presenting a public Muslim self promoted by the mosque had its own internal logic—that of presenting a corrective and sympathetic image of Islam to non-Muslims—it also ran head-on into the carefully forged and daily lived model of Muslim youth identity that had emerged from the Legendz's years together, one that was informed by powerful urban American cultural expectations of autonomy, "normalcy," and self-defense. In short, the mosque leadership's model of the ideal Muslim youth was no match for the durability of the model formed by the small group and its repeatedly reinforced core cultural components of low-key Islam, American teenage capacities, and demonstrated autonomy. The Legendz's model of public American selfhood, grounded in responses to the group's everyday realities and forged in a dense thicket of mutual interactions, reflected more closely the daily experiences of these urban Muslim American young men. For this reason, their method for presenting a Muslim self in public proved a better cultural fit for them than did the one developed by mosque leaders.

6

Growing Up Muslim and American

First of all, regarding this question of, "Are we Muslim or American?," we should not allow this question. You are Muslim American. Islam is not a geographical or ethnic identity. Wherever I land, even if I landed on the moon, I would be a Muslim on the moon. I have a mandate wherever I live to live as Muslim. Youth are Muslim Americans. You have to be comfortable with your religion and also proud of your country. This is the only country that gave you the best opportunity to make a difference. [. . .] But the adults sometimes expect the impossible of youth, to ask them to have a dual personality. So we tell them things like, "When you come to the mosque, wear the hijab, but after that, do whatever you like." This is devastating. We have to open ourselves to the youth as they are and work with them to get where we should be. Otherwise, we give them an example of hypocrisy. People who grow up in America have a strong revulsion towards hypocrisy. Being brought up in the US, I'm trying to be myself, to be who I am. When I was growing up it was, "Act this way or what will they think of us?" I don't care what they say about you. I want you to evolve in a healthy way that gives me happiness. Islam wants you to be happy and cheerful, not miserable.

—DR. RAMSEY MUBARAK, SPEAKING TO CITY MOSQUE YOUTH, DECEMBER 20, 2009

Muslim American youth are American teenagers and thus share the concerns of most other American adolescents: music, being "cool," dating and romance, independence and autonomy, fitting in, and standing up for themselves. More than that, Muslim teenagers share with other American young people the ongoing predicament of living culturally contested lives, a situation in which competing sets of cultural expectations, each of which is associated with a socially significant group or identity, vie for attention and commitment in their daily lives. Just as other teens may work to balance participation in "jock" and "burnout" crowds, "good" and "ghetto" styles, home and host country cultures, or religious and secular activities, Muslim American teenagers seek to manage their involvement in both youthful American and religiously Islamic modes of social and cultural life.

The specific ways in which Muslim American young men work to strike this balance reveal further similarities between Muslim youth and other young people in the United States, as many of the particular strategies and practices they employ are comparable to those used by other kinds of youth facing cultural complexity. For example, Muslim youth participate in youth-associated pop culture and recreational activities in strategic ways aimed at obtaining an aura of "cool" while still avoiding involvement in actually deviant or dangerous behavior. This attempt to engage in popular styles while "skirting the border" of inappropriate action is a common tactic among African American youth growing up in American cities, white teenagers attending large public schools in US suburbs, and young second-generation immigrants seeking to fit in in America without losing their sense of ethnic identity.[1] In particular, the flexibility and social resonance of "category symbols"[2] such as musical genres and lyrics, fashion and clothing, and slang and physical gestures enable young people from these diverse social contexts to experience and project a youthful American "coolness," even if many or most of their behaviors and commitments still lie within the realm of local communal acceptability.

Another familiar way in which Muslim American young men respond to their situation of cultural contestation is by relying on discourses and performances of American individualism amid everyday communal (and, in their case, Islamic) obligations. This strategy allows them to emphasize a symbolic distance between their independent young selves and the communally rooted cultural expectations of their parents and religious tradition. Such use of individualistic language and behavior to underscore independence in the midst of social obligation has also been seen among a range of subsets of American youth, including white working-class youth seeking to distance themselves from the institution of school and expectations of normative academic achievement and highly religious youth positioning themselves as separable from overarching doctrine and tradition.[3] One particular practice of discursive individualism common to all of these groups is the repeated interactional invocation of an "extreme" caricature of the unthinking, traditionally static, and culturally bound community member from whom youth wish to differentiate themselves.[4] The popularity of this practice shows how the establishment of an identity as a young, individualistic American in everyday interaction is fundamentally a *relational* process, as it often relies on the invocation of crude stereotypes of static tradition, ethnicity, or religion to which one's own dynamic individualism can be favorably compared.

The everyday lives of Muslim American young men reveal other patterned strategies, also similar to those used by various kinds of American young people to manage their culturally contested lives. Like teenagers growing up in evangelical Christian or traditionally Catholic communities, Muslim American young men sometimes seek to participate in romantic relationships in ways that adhere to guidelines drawn by religious tradition and sometimes date in ways that ignore such communal norms.[5] Young American Muslims occasionally downplay their minority identity in the public sphere in order to ease social acceptance, a strategy also seen among working-class white and Latino teenagers, African American youth from poor neighborhoods, and second-generation immigrant youth.[6] And, like most American teenagers, Muslim young men work to cultivate and demonstrate skills in locally valued activities— playing and performing music, excelling in certain sports, or engaging in physical fighting—in an attempt to fit in with and be accepted by their school or neighborhood peer group.[7]

What these deeply patterned similarities between the culturally contested situations and strategic solutions of Muslim and other American youth strongly suggest is that Muslim American teenagers like those described in this book are fundamentally *American teenagers*, experiencing and navigating Islamically inflected versions of the same cultural contradictions and identity navigation processes familiar to other young people living in the United States. Considering Muslim American youth as American teenagers pushes us, in looking at Muslim teenagers, to foreground the issues and challenges faced by all young people living culturally contested lives rather than seeking out an exclusively "Muslim" or "Islamic" set of issues or concerns. Such a perspective—seeing Muslim youth as teenagers first—allows us to, in the words of sociologist Sami Zubaida, look "beyond Islam" when considering Muslim American youth.[8] By tempering the expectation that something "Muslim" or "Islamic"—and therefore something fundamentally *different*—must lie at the heart of the identity or daily experiences of Muslim American youth, we can look at Muslim young men in ways that allow the many other typical issues they face, such as romantic relationships, concerns for social acceptance, and the desire for independence, to come to the fore. An acknowledgment of the fundamental American teenageness of Muslim American youth can actually grant us a clearer, more accurate view of these young people *as* Muslim youth, because it will allow us to consider Islamic expectations, discourses, and practices alongside and intertwined with more "typical" teenage concerns. In this way, we may come to see and understand Muslim American young people for what they truly are, instead of what we may fear, hope, or desire them to be.

The Legendz Three and Five Years Later

I have conducted two "follow-up visits" with the Legendz since leaving the City Mosque and ending my main period of fieldwork in June 2010. The goals of these visits were, first, to check in on the Legendz's lives in general and, second, to assess whether and how issues related to the management of culturally contested lives remained relevant to their young adult realities. My first visit consisted of a three-day trip to Coast City in August 2013, during which I spent time with the boys at their jobs, their homes, and the mosque. This trip allowed me to witness in-group dynamics and to speak with some of them one on one. The second "visit" was actually virtual, as I conducted in-depth interviews with five of the Legendz over Skype in January and February of 2015 in order to catch up on their lives and ask them a few follow-up questions.

These visits left me with two impressions relevant to the core themes of this book. First, I found that as the Legendz moved further away from the tight-knit community of their mosque and families and into other social domains such as work and college, the culturally contested nature of their lives became less pronounced, and the need to actively manage participation in different cultural rubrics was reduced. Second, I discovered that as the boys entered the stage of life commonly known as "young adulthood," the influence of their religious community and families became less direct and binding, and the strategic cultural reconciliation that had occupied so much of their earlier adolescence seemed less urgent and relevant.

This did not mean, however, that the cultural rubric of religious Islam was completely absent from their lives. On the contrary, despite the fact that cultural contestation seemed less important to the Legendz in 2013, I also observed that the practices, ideas, and discourses of religious Islam remained present in their daily lives and speech. The Legendz still clearly considered themselves Muslims and thought about their everyday endeavors from an Islamic perspective, but this no longer seemed to require as much active negotiation as it had when they were younger. Indeed, by this point, typical American young adult activities (dating, going out at night, some drinking) and Islamic identity and practice seemed to coexist in their daily lives, with little apparent need for reconciliation or resolution. This dual reality—the Legendz's move away from a more intensive concern with reconciling Islam with young adult practices and their acceptance of the fact that certain elements of Islam could coexist with these practices—was the main finding of my follow-up time with them. What it says about this later stage of their lives and what it might portend for the future are the subjects of this chapter.

In 2013, when I visited the Legendz for a long weekend, all of the boys (save Salman, who was seventeen) had entered their twenties and were involved in some combination of work and college.[9] Yusef was finishing up his final classes at a state university while working full time at an engineering firm. He told me that he didn't like the job that much because he found it too "isolating." Muhammad was still working at the front desk of the mosque and was taking classes at Coast City Community College. Abdul was "second in charge" at a valet company, which involved supervising valets at three different restaurants in the downtown area, including Downtown Hookah, a place I had heard the Legendz mention before. Abdul told me that he liked the job because it was challenging and interesting but also said that his boss made him deal with a lot of stressful "bullshit." Abdul was also enrolled in classes at Coast City Community College and said he was choosing between a major in business or premed. Tariq worked as a driver for the same valet company as Abdul did, at a restaurant not far from Downtown Hookah. Salman was still in high school and heavily into skateboarding and music.

The Legendz's movement into young adulthood meant that their daily lives were now organized around college and work rather than high school, the mosque, and their families. The Legendz were now spending more time in social settings *not* clearly associated with the cultural rubric of Islam than they had in their high school and early college years. The fact that both Abdul and Tariq had jobs downtown and that the other kids liked to go to this area meant that the group spent a significant amount of social time in a part of the city known for its bars, clubs, and nightlife, and specifically at Downtown

Hookah. On the first day of my visit, which happened to fall during the last week of Ramadan, I went with the boys to the mosque for a fast-breaking dinner (iftar) and then to Downtown Hookah so that I could see where they worked and spent much of their days. From the moment we began our car ride downtown, it became clear that dating, relationships with some physical intimacy, and urban nightlife were now far more central to the Legendz's social world than they had been three years earlier.

We walk to Yusef's car and start driving downtown. From the backseat, Muhammad says, "My friend Ali's going on this date and the girl says, 'I want to bring my sister, can you bring a friend?' So he asked me, and the sister is *fine*!" Yusef laughs and says, "Let's see a picture of the sister!" Muhammad says, "Alright, let me get it on Instagram for you." Later he says, "Argh, it doesn't work on Instagram. . . ." Abdul says, "What ethnicity are they?" "Indonesian," says Muhammad. We drive down Central Ave. Salman, who has joined us for the ride, says, "Yeah, I need to talk to some girls tonight." Yusef says, "No, you guys, we shouldn't be thinking about this stuff right now. It's the last six days of Ramadan. I mean, think about it, these are the six most important days of the whole year. We shouldn't get distracted by that stuff right now." Everyone else in the car nods quietly.

We pull up in front of the Downtown Hookah Lounge on Prentiss Boulevard. Yusef pulls to the curb and we all get out. As he will continue to do for the rest of the night, Abdul introduces me to everyone he knows at the place: the valet workers, the waitresses, the head of the valet company, the owner of the lounge, etc. The waitresses all look very young, in their very early twenties at most, and look similar to each other. They wear very short black dresses and have long black hair. They are all very friendly with Abdul, Yusef, Muhammad, and Tariq, who comes later. We sit down on one of the couches and order two hookahs. Muhammad and Abdul walk into the back and talk to the guys who mix the hookahs. They do this on and off occasionally throughout the night. Salman seems nervous as we sit down, and he's talking to

Yusef. "What's going on?" I ask them. Yusef looks at me, half-smiling, and says quietly: "You're supposed to be twenty-one to be in here." "Oh," I say. Salman says, "I'm seventeen." Abdul, sitting to Salman's left, says, "So if the cops come, we have to take him out the back." "Oh," I say. "You've never been here before?" Salman shakes his head "no" back and forth. One of the waitresses comes and brings two hookahs to our table and puts hot coals on top. After she leaves, Salman says to Yusef, "These waiters are the bomb." Yusef smiles and says to him, "Waitresses." "Oh yeah," Salman says, "waitresses." Yusef says, with only the slightest hint of condescension, "Waiters are men."

The cafe is dark but not too dark, with hip hop from about five years ago playing loudly and television screens fixed to the walls all around us. Smoke rises from various hookahs at the surrounding tables, and when no one is talking, it's easy to let your attention drift to the video screen and get caught up in the flow of beat and lyrics. We sit, smoke, and talk for a while. Abdul tells me in some detail about some of the romantic and sexual exploits of the boys. He also tells me that he had seriously dated an Egyptian Muslim girl for about a year. "But then she wanted to get married, and I wasn't trying to do that. So she left me for a thirty-year-old engineer." "Wow, seriously?" I ask. "Yeah," he says.

Later in the night, I walk out in front of the lounge with Yusef. As we stand and talk, we watch as increasing numbers of obviously drunk people spill out of the many nearby nightclubs and onto the street. There are a lot of scantily dressed women either with men or being aggressively hit on by men. Couples make out on the street. Tariq shows up and, at one point, poses for a lot of pictures with one of the waitresses in front of the lounge. I can't figure out if they are romantically involved or not. Yusef says he needs to go home and take care of a couple of things, so he calls for his car. As I stand waiting with him, more women in short and tight clothing walk by. At one point, after we both turn our heads to look, Yusef says, "We need to say a lot of Astaghfirullah [God forgive me!] tonight." I smile.

My time spent with the Legendz in 2013 showed me how at this point in the boys' lives, hanging out downtown at night, sexual exploration, intensive dating, and some drinking were all part of their social lives. This does not mean that they never spent time at the mosque or in their families' homes. The boys all still lived with their parents, and the mosque was still a place where they attended Jummah prayer and community events. But their center of gravity had certainly shifted from the settings of the mosque, home, and neighborhood to college, work, downtown, the hookah lounge, and nightlife destinations. Abdul referred to this as the boys' "experimental period."

On the first afternoon of my visit, before going to the Downtown Hookah lounge, I sat with Abdul and Muhammad in the familiar setting of the MYP room at the City Mosque. As we caught up on news, Muhammad expressed his disappointment at the new direction and leadership of the mosque's youth program. He claimed that it was no longer as fun as it used to be, and that they had stopped holding retreats and ski trips because some kids had been caught "smoking weed" during one of the trips. At this point I asked:

> "Aren't there people who say that smoking weed isn't haram?" "Yeah," Muhammad says. "But I don't even think that's a good argument. I mean, I've smoked a little, I've drunk a little." Abdul says, "Yeah, we're all having our experimental period." "But did you guys do any of that stuff in high school?" I ask. "No." They both shake their heads. "But something about college," Abdul says, "is more like time for your experimental period. . . . You'll see some when you come downtown with us."

Later that afternoon, Abdul and I went on a walk behind the mosque, and I took the opportunity to ask him more about this shift in behavior.

> "So everybody's been going through a college experimental phase?" "Yeah," he says. "I've been drinking a little. I don't get wasted, you know. Just have a couple of drinks after work or something. I don't like it that much. And I've had some short

things with some girls. But I've never done any of the hard stuff, like cocaine and heroin, and I've seen a lot of that. But I'm definitely staying away from that! But there's something about college that people are experimenting a little bit."

Abdul's labeling of this period of the Legendz's lives—in which they engaged in overt dating, occasional drinking, and some drug use—as an "experimental period" could be seen here as a strategy for making these activities appear less serious or consequential and less at odds with the competing expectations associated with his identity as a practicing Muslim. In this sense, Abdul's comments might have been a way for him to frame this behavior *to me*—an older, practicing Muslim adult—as something that had a temporal endpoint and therefore should not be overly concerning vis-à-vis his status as a "good" Muslim. It is also worth noting, and is in keeping with our consideration of the Legendz as American young people, that treating the post–high school years as a bracketed time period in which young people engage in behavior that they did not participate in formerly and may not participate in later in life is a common practice among young American adults.[10]

In terms of this study, what is significant about the Legendz's "experimental period" is the particular ways in which they consistently intermixed the behaviors of this phase—which were generally considered haram by the Legendz's community and were strongly associated with American young adult culture—with idioms, frameworks, and modes of thought drawn from religious Islam. It was Yusef who brought considerations of Islam into the conversation during my visit to the hookah lounge recounted earlier, first by reminding the others (and himself) that they should not think too much about girls that night because it was the last six days of Ramadan, "the six most important days of the whole year," and later, as we were both drawn to watching women with revealing clothes, by stating, "We need to say a lot of Astaghfirullah [God forgive me!] tonight."

During my visit with the Legendz, the other boys used Islamic frameworks and ideas in similar ways. As I sat and talked with Muhammad and Abdul at the mosque before our night out downtown, I asked Muhammad what people thought about the religious permissiveness of smoking hookah:

> I ask them, "But what about hookah? Does anyone say that's haram?" Muhammad says, "Not really. But none of it is good for you. I mean, smoke is just bad for you. It deteriorates your body. But I don't think it needs to be about haram and halal. It's more like, if the Qur'an says that your body is from Allah and it will return to him, then you need to take care of it. Your body is a temple, you know. So any kind of smoke is bad for that— cigarettes are bad for that. . . . So that's how I think people should think about it."

While Muhammad did not come down too strongly on the issue of smoking hookah, he did draw on an Islamic framework to support his opinion by referencing the Qur'an. Similarly, when Abdul told me about his "experimental phase" during our walk, he also confessed:

> "I haven't been to the mosque in a while." "Really?" I say. "Yeah," he says. "Probably for a few months. . . . This really hasn't been the most spiritual month of my year. I've been messing around, going to bars with random chicks sometimes, stuff like that. I don't know what I'm doing."

As the boys moved deeper into experimenting with intimate relationships, alcohol, and nightlife recreation in their young adult years, the cultural rubric of Islam remained present, if more muted, as a set of interpretative tools through which they could view these activities, even when they did not end up acting on the understanding of what was Islamically appropriate. The boys did not use religious and cultural Islam as a means to pass final judgment on these actions, nor did they attempt to reconcile Islam with American young adult culture. As in the "dating while Muslim" approach to romantic relationships, an unresolved and open-ended co-presence of religious Islam and American youth culture was maintained in everyday life.

What is impossible to tell from my brief visit with the Legendz in 2013 is whether the discourses and considerations of Islamic morality that were present during my visit were raised by Yusef, Muhammad, and Abdul primarily *in response to my presence*—in order to reassure me, a close Muslim adult friend, that they were still "good" Muslims despite their other activities that may have suggested otherwise—or if this language reflected a deeper, real, and perhaps more anguished concern with how Islamic expectations for behavior related to their young adult lives and activities. While I am unable to know the answer for sure, what I can say with confidence is that—whether in response to my presence or not—the Legendz did maintain a *familiarity and facility* with discourses from and references to religious Islam, a cache of cultural symbols that Daniel Brown has referred to as Islam's "common grammar."[11] Whether or not the Legendz felt beholden to the Islamic ideas of propriety that still lived within their heads, memories, and everyday speech, they still *knew* them, and this knowledge represented a still-active link to their Muslim identities, one they could express together. Precisely what their ongoing familiarity and facility with this common grammar of Islam meant for the Legendz, their Muslim identity, and their sense of religiosity through the years was impossible to ascertain at the time.

THE FUTURE OF THE LEGENDZ

One reason why it was difficult to predict exactly where the Legendz's trajectories of identity, religiosity, and selfhood were headed was that at the time of my visit they were undergoing a significant stage of transition, a phase of life known as "emerging adulthood."[12] In this stage, as young people move ever further from the direct control of their families and secondary schools, they often wrestle more openly and intensely with issues of identity and life direction. These topics were clearly on the minds of the Legendz during the follow-up interviews I conducted with them in early 2015. Emanating a palpable sense of restlessness, Yusef told me that he was strongly considering a move to the opposite coast for a while in order to "get to know myself a little more . . . get my mind off of things around here, just kind of go and be on my own for a little while, like, really be on my own, like, really far away . . . yeah, establish myself and come back a better man." On the one hand, he sounded as though he was experiencing a common young adult desire to spend some time "finding himself." On the other hand, this need to move away seemed related to the specific ways in which his life up to that point had been fairly constrained by family and community expectations.

> I just want to go out and, like, do my own thing and, like . . . build myself up. Because I feel like I'll have a better sense of accomplishment then. You know, and that's just me, I mean. . . . I just don't want to be around family. I just don't want to be around anybody that can . . . that thinks they have some kind of authority over me, you know. . . . And I just don't want . . . I don't want to deal with that . . . for . . . for now.

Salman, who was also a responsible eldest brother with highly religious parents, expressed similar sentiments and told me that he too was considering going to college in a city far away.

> I've been wanting to go there . . . for years. . . . I'm still doing research on how to find a way to, you know, get there from here. . . . Oh, man, I want to try something different. I haven't really traveled before. I've just been in this city my whole life, so I think just having an opportunity to travel and just to live a different lifestyle and, I don't know, just, like, gaining a better . . . you know, like a bigger perspective. I feel that'll just be good for myself . . . you know.

These plans to move away from family and community are significant to understanding the continuing story of the Legendz. For one, they indicate that while time spent in intensive interaction with members of the same cultural community may be a means of cultivating a workable multicultural selfhood, it can also result in a feeling of being socially hemmed in. Both Yusef and Salman had spent sufficient time inside the small group incubator of their friendship group, nested within the mosque and community, to have gained a durable sense of themselves as both Muslims and Americans. By 2015, however, they were articulating a desire to escape from this very setting because of the limitations and constraints it had imposed on them.

More directly relevant to the question of the trajectory of the Leg-endz's ongoing process of cultural navigation is the impact that a move away from the community might have on the boys' sense of them-selves as Muslims and Americans. As Yusef and Salman considered moving and Muhammad, Abdul, and Tariq, who remained closer to home, grew increasingly involved in locally "un-Islamic" activities, how would their relationships to religious Islam and American cultural rubrics change, if at all? As mentioned earlier, it was impossible to predict the answer to this question with any certainty. What I could do, however, was to consider what I knew of the Legendz and other cases like theirs and sketch out the *potential* directions their paths might take vis-à-vis issues of identity, religiosity, and selfhood.

One possibility was that because the Legendz had been effec-tively inculcated with the ability to experience the cultural rubrics of religious Islam and American youth culture in concert they would be able to carry this combination of Islamic and American cultural tools—accompanied by a sense of Muslim American identity—with them to their new social destinations: college, work, and urban nightlife. This possible outcome, which finds common ground with the theories of cultural socialization put forward by sociologists Pierre Bourdieu and Ann Swidler, assigns great power to the pro-cesses of developing "cultured capacities,"[13] or sets of dispositions[14] that remain influential throughout our lives, even if their particular applications vary according to the social situation. Following the logic of these theorists, I could hypothesize that the Legendz would maintain a strong sense of both Muslim and American identity as they moved further into independent adulthood, and that their abil-ity to manage participation in both rubrics would continue to gener-ate workable modes of multicultural selfhood.

Another trajectory was possible, however. As the Legendz moved further away from settings dominated by Islamic culture or a blend of Islamic and American cultures into those dominated by different types of more broadly "American" culture, they might no longer experience strong social expectations for participation in either Muslim or Muslim American ways of life. As the immediate social significance and ac-companying social pressure of participation in religious Islam faded, so too might the Legendz's engagement in Islam as a cultural rubric and, as a consequence, their experience of Muslim American subjectivity. This outcome would find support from a strain of research—now somewhat dated but still influential in terms of conventional thinking about religious youth—that indicates that when young religious people enter young adulthood, and especially go to college, their religious belief, identity, and practice dramatically decline.[15]

A third possible trajectory, similar to the first in terms of outcome, considers the potential importance of continuing peer and family influence. Even if the Legendz moved away from more "Islamic" settings, they might maintain ongoing relationships with and links to Muslim friends and family via social media, visits, and friends of friends. Thus, a continuing, albeit looser, "plausibility structure" of Muslim American subjectivity might still exert sufficient power to keep Islam relevant to their lives. If this proved to be the case, the Legendz might maintain an engagement with Islamic practice and identity and continue to see this as compatible with their American identity even as they moved into nominally non-Islamic social settings.

My observations of the Legendz in high school as well as my later visits strongly suggest this outcome: that the powerful lessons that they learned from their time spent together as adolescents, reinforced by their continuing social connections to Muslim friends and family, will sustain in these young men a lasting sense of Muslim American identity. While only time will tell whether my prediction proves correct, my firsthand witness of the intensive strategies and complex commitments lived out by the Legendz during their teen and early adult years leads me to believe that they are particularly well suited to continue inhabiting varying and flexible yet persistent and ongoing manifestations of Muslim American identity though their adult years and beyond.

Growing up Muslim and American

Since I embarked on this project nearly ten years ago, isolated cases of troubled young Muslim men in the "West" have gained massive attention from the media and law enforcement. From stories of young Muslims planning to leave the United States to join the so-called Islamic State to the case of Orlando shooter Omar Mateen, these highly visible but still exceedingly rare cases of young Muslim Americans, who often seemed to have struggled with issues of identity and belonging, have led colleagues, journalists, and policymakers to ask me, "Can young Muslims grow up in America with a healthy sense of their identity?" At the same time, personal friends and acquaintances who have heard about this project, as well as parents of Muslim youth in the United States, have repeatedly asked me, "How can we raise young Muslims in America in a way that they can keep their Muslim and American identities intact?" Although these questions are motivated by different concerns, I believe that the main findings of this book offer answers to both questions as well as guidance about positive ways in which young Muslims can grow up in America with minimal social or cultural strife.

The case of the Legendz and the City Mosque shows that in early twenty-first-century America it is clearly possible for young Muslim men, given the right conditions, to express and experience a workable, subjective sense of Muslim American selfhood. While the young men in this book certainly faced challenges in navigating their culturally contested lives, they approached these situations as manageable dilemmas, practical predicaments that they could deal with, rather than overwhelming or stressful crises. These young people eventually considered cultural practices of religious Islam and American youth culture as strands that could be woven together, kept apart, or considered in relation to each other, but *not as essentially or irrevocably in conflict*. While the case of the Legendz is but one example of Muslim American youth, I believe that their story suggests key conditions important to the cultivation of healthy Muslim American identities more broadly.

The Legendz's deep and pervasive sense of themselves as Muslims and Americans, as well as their cultivated ability to skillfully navigate the cultural rubrics of American youth culture and Islamic religiosity, are attributable to three key conditions present within their social environment. First, the adults in the Legendz's community maintained an openness and understanding that allowed the boys room to engage in some measure of American youth culture without fear of harsh punishment or communal ostracism. Their religious director, Omar, Dr. Mubarak, and youth leader Melvin all drew the line at behaviors they considered antithetical to core Islamic principles but did not react harshly when members of the Legendz participated to some degree in mainstream youth culture by listening to hip hop or expressing romantic interest in young women. Instead of simply denouncing what the boys were doing as haram, these adults often turned such issues into subjects of conversation, consideration, and debate from an Islamic perspective. These adults' power in relation to the youth meant that they played a crucial role in defining which behavior was or was not deemed egregious enough to threaten a young person's social standing within the family, tradition, or community.[16] When adults in a community understand that youth behavior is often symbolic, strategic, and part of an ongoing process rather than a definite and final statement aimed at refuting one's ethnic or religious heritage, they are more likely to provide young people with adequate room to attempt cultural navigations than to instinctively clamp down or stifle what may be developmentally important moments of identity exploration.

A second important condition seems to have been the presence of a familiar and consistent group of friends located within the same culturally complex situation. The Legendz developed a sense of their ability to manage competing sets of cultural expectations as young Muslims *together*. They helped each other to develop an understanding of the precise challenges they faced and to cultivate and apply practical strategies for managing their culturally contested lives. The central importance of the friendship group for the navigation of culturally contested lives that I observed in the Legendz's case also finds support in the work of social psychologists, who have emphasized the importance of small groups for in-group culture creation; sociologists of youth, who have demonstrated the power of peer-to-peer socialization; and sociologists of race and ethnicity, who have argued for the importance of similarly socially situated peers for the development of positive identity.[17] The Legendz too seemed to recognize their importance to one another as allies in navigating their culturally contested situations. When I spoke with Salman in 2015 about his experience growing up as part of the Legendz, he talked effusively about the impact of the other boys on both him and other young people at the mosque:

> I feel like, you know, Abdul, and Muhammad and everyone did something. . . . They just kept being themselves. . . . And honestly, that's what drove more people to come to the youth group. . . . And, like, I remember kids would come, like . . . I don't know how to describe it. They come in very like . . . like they're not *hatched*. Like they have so much that they want to expose. They want to really free themselves. But, you know, because of parents and because of their . . . their current situation, they're just . . . they don't know how to hatch, you know . . . from their shells. But I feel like a lot of these kids, being around, you know, a lot of the people that are around us, around Abdul, and Muhammad, and Yusef, and just our group, you know . . . they're kind of able to learn how to hatch themselves and just kind of be the people they want to be. Like just be free! That's the best way I can describe it.

A third condition that seems to have contributed to the Legendz's ability to effectively manage their culturally contested lives was a social and physical space in which these processes could unfold and take place. For the Legendz, this space obviously included the mosque, but it also extended to the availability of areas officially on the mosque's property but outside of the close watch of adults. The back parking lot, the social hall on a quiet late afternoon, the youth room after official meetings were over, and the main lobby late at night all served as arenas where religious Islam was present and relevant but not dominant or authoritative, where elements of youth culture and religious culture could playfully intermix without immediate sanction, and where the Legendz could experience first-hand the possibility of a nonconflicting coexistence of Islamic and youth cultural elements and practices. The significant role played by the mosque and its proximate spaces falls in line with observations made by sociologists of immigration on the importance of immigrant institutions and organizations as places where healthy processes of acculturation and adaptation can take place.[18] This suggests that one way to support the ability of young Muslims to develop a sense of themselves as both Muslim and American is to advocate for spaces within mosques, Islamic centers, and Muslim communities at large in which young people's concerns, needs, and desires can be more openly taken into account and given room for expression and exploration.

An underlying theme cutting across all three of these conditions—openness on the part of adults, the presence of young Muslim peers who share the same cultural context, and social and physical space—is the need for a productive overall understanding of Muslim American teenagers as being *in the midst of a process* of identity development, cultural negotiation, and growing up. If young Muslims are granted space within their communities to allow such processes to unfold, with guidance offered when necessary, then they can effectively work with one another to make sense of their culturally contested lives. But the work to be done should not fall exclusively on the shoulders of Muslims and Muslim youth in their own communities. All of us must be open to seeing Muslim American youth as young people who are engaged in processes of social, psychological, and identity development—in other words, as American teenagers. To do this is to recognize that, in the ways in which they desire to keep various possibilities alive and open, seek ways to partake in both the familiar warmth of cultural tradition and the excitement and rush of personal freedom, and strive to fit in while maintaining a sense of their own individuality, Muslim American youth are not only fundamentally similar to other American young people, but profoundly similar to all Americans.

APPENDIX: THE LEGENDZ

Abdul: Ages 16–19; Jordanian American; younger brother of Yusef; "dated while Muslim."

Abshir: Ages 15–18; Somali American; liked to play football; didn't like to pray on time.

Fuad: Ages 14–17; Sudanese American; younger brother of Muhammad; best friends with Abdul; always dressed well.

Muhammad: Ages 17–20; Sudanese American; older brother of Fuad; best friends with Yusef; loved hip hop.

Salman: Ages 11–14; South Asian American; "younger cousin" of the group; loved skateboarding; romantic and religious "idealist."

Tariq: Ages 14–17; South Asian American; played basketball to fit in; the "quiet one."

Yusef: Ages 17–20; Jordanian American; older brother of Abdul; best friends with Muhammad; called "the imam."

ACKNOWLEDGMENTS

This book could not have been written without a tremendous amount of support, encouragement, and guidance from a wide array of wonderful people over the past many years. I am deeply grateful to them all, and I will try to express that gratitude here. First and foremost, to the Legendz: thank you for letting me into your lives and for giving me the chance to tell your story. I am still struck by the trust and generosity you demonstrated by allowing me into your circle, and I hope I have represented you truthfully and well. I'll never forget the time we spent together, and I count you all as lifelong friends. I miss you guys! Also, to the City Mosque community: I am deeply grateful for your openness and patience, as well as for your support of this project. I especially want to single out "Omar Hashmi," the religious director, and the friend in common who introduced us, for your essential contributions to making this project possible.

I was incredibly fortunate to have the brilliant, funny, and always focused Stefan Timmermans as my main advisor while in graduate school at the University of California, Los Angeles (UCLA), when this project was first started as my PhD dissertation. Stefan was invaluable in his steadfast encouragement for the topic, in his incisive recommendations about my research and writing, and for showing me that it was possible to be both a responsible parent and a committed ethnographer. Because of Stefan, I am a Timmermaniac through and through. The three other professors on my dissertation committee also provided crucial inspiration and guidance. Bill Roy pushed me to think comparatively in rigorous ways and to consider the role of "audience" in interactions, and was always there when I needed a word of encouragement or advice. Rogers Brubaker's commitment to avoiding facile "groupness" and constant reminders to analytically "disaggregate" helped challenge my thinking in fruitful ways. And Paul Lichterman provided crucial insight into my thinking about the everyday workings of religion and culture at a point when I needed some inspiration and direction. This book is much stronger for the input of these thoughtful and generous mentors.

I was fortunate to have attended graduate school with a group of smart, diverse, and energetic young scholars, many of whom challenged my thinking and provided me with support in important and meaningful ways. Laura Orrico was always around for a thoughtful talk and a laugh when I needed a boost. Forrest Stuart inspired me with his rare and wonderful mix of sociological fervor and down-to-earth perspective. Fellow young ethnographers in the department provided me with models for doing the work as well as templates for how to think about it in reflective and effective ways; they included Iddo Tavory, Jooyoung Lee, Rocio Rosales, Nazgol Gandnoosh, David Trouille, Mike DeLand, and other members of the Ethnography Working Group. Other cohort-mates as well as UCLA Sociology students in years below and above me gave me an exciting intellectual home as well as a feeling of family. Among them were Anthony Ocampo, Anthony Alvarez, Chinyere Osuji, Zeynep Ozgen, Rob Jansen, Pamela Prickett, Gabriel Nelson, Yuval Feinstein, Yana Kucheva, Dwight Davis, Jenjira Yahirun, Sylvia Zamora, Molly Jacobs, Caitlin Patler, Kjerstin Gruys, Sarah Morando Lakhani, William Rosales, Elena Shih, Tara McKay, Gustav Brown, Phillipe Duart, Erika Arenas, Noriko Milman, Marie Berry, Hyeyoung Oh, and Anup Sheth. I still carry with me the model of collegiality and intellectual community that I learned during those UCLA days.

Over the almost ten years of working on this project, there were many points at which I reached out to more experienced sociologists who gave me a small piece of advice or word of encouragement that made a big difference in the course of this book. For this crucial kind of help, I want to thank Claudio Benzecry, Courtney Bender, Gary Alan Fine, Rhys Williams, Natasha Warikoo, Ellen Berrey, Tim Dowd, Gerardo Marti, Colin Jerolmack, Dalton Conley,

David Grazian, Steve Warner, Bob Wuthnow, Jennifer Lena, Michele Lamont, Andrew Deener, Peggy Levitt, Monica McDermott, and Matt Wray. During this same period, I was fortunate enough to make connections with young sociologists who were brave enough to still believe that religion is something we need to understand and study within sociology. I thank them for their thoughtful e-mail exchanges, enthusiastic chats at conferences, and just being out there. Besheer Mohamed, Courtney Irby, Ruth Braunstein, Jeff Guhin, Rachel Rinaldo, Daniel Winchester, Alison Denton Jones, Michal Pagis, Lydia Bean, Todd Nicholas Fuist, Orit Avishai, Graham Hill, and Brandon Vaidyanathan, your work on religion inspires me and gives me hope for deepening our understanding of this phenomenon that still means so much to so many.

This book was finished during my first years as an assistant professor of sociology at New York University Abu Dhabi (NYUAD) in the United Arab Emirates. NYUAD has been a wonderful home institution for me, thanks to the presence of smart and supportive colleagues, bright and stimulating students, and an administration that values both research and good teaching. I could not have asked for a more supportive and encouraging department head than Hannah Brüeckner during these years. Hannah has provided me with far more mentorship, guidance, and understanding than I ever could have expected in this early stage of my career, and I am deeply grateful to her for everything she has done for me. I was also fortunate to arrive at NYUAD when Ivan Szelenyi was the dean of social sciences. While heading up this small but growing academic division, Ivan found the time to provide me with doses of sage advice, strategic wisdom, and good humor, all when I needed them most. Hervé Crès, who followed Ivan as dean, has expressed an enthusiastic confidence and trust in me that helped me to finish the project. Within the department, I have been honored and privileged to work alongside Daniel Karrel, May Al Dabbagh, Elisabeth Anderson, Swethaa Ballakrishnen, Georgi Derlugyan, Zeynep Ozgen, Allen Li, and Peter Stamatov. Providing important inspiration and practical help for me during this time were two students, Eman Ebdalhadi, a graduate student at NYU in New York, and Lotus Mohajer, an undergraduate senior at NYU Abu Dhabi. Finally, senior colleagues from NYU in New York and other US universities who have come to Abu Dhabi to visit have proven to be wonderful mentors. My thanks to Ann Morning, Harvey Molotch, Jeff Manza, Roger Friedland, Alejandro Portes, and especially the irreplaceable Paula England for playing this important role in my early career.

Once the book started to take shape, I needed to find a publisher. My heartfelt thanks to Professor Peter Bearman—who was visiting NYU Abu Dhabi at the time—for helping me to make a connection with Princeton University Press. Once the book was at Princeton, Fred Appel lived up to his reputation as a thoughtful, considerate, and thorough editor, guiding me through the editorial process and helping me to turn a fledgling dissertation into what is (I hope) a more cogent, readable, and incisive book. Fred has been the perfect editor for this project, and I am fortunate to have had such an experienced guide at such an esteemed publisher. Irina Oryshkevich and Sarah Vogelsong provided wonderful editing to get the manuscript in shape for publication. Parts of chapter 2 were previously published as "Muslim Youth and Secular Hip Hop: Manifesting 'Cool Piety' Through Musical Practices" in *Poetics* 41:99–121 in 2013. Thanks to *Poetics* for their permission.

Special thanks to one of my sociological heroes, Mitch Duneier, who took the time to read and give feedback on an earlier draft of the manuscript, and whose support and encouragement for this project have been crucial. Mitch's model of how to "show the people" in ethnography and his steadfast commitment to analytical rigor in qualitative research are an inspiration. I hope I can reflect but a small part of his ethnographic skill and sociological imagination in my own work. I also want to express my deep gratitude to Susan Smulyan, my undergraduate advisor in American Studies at Brown University, for teaching me how to take the everyday concerns and passions of "ordinary" people seriously as an important subject of study, research, and understanding. I am forever in Susan's debt for this invaluable lesson.

Over the course of the writing process, wonderful friends too have provided me with important moral support and kindness.

Those who have been there with an encouraging word, help with childcare, or a delicious baked good include Jeff Jensen and Christina Zenker, Justin Stearns and Nathalie Puetz, Cyrus Patell and Deborah Williams, Andy and Rachel Harris, Rachel Brulé and Michael Harsch, Matty Silverstein and Roberta Wertman, and Bryan and Stephanie Waterman. Old friends from previous lives kept me sane and supported on Skype calls, WhatsApp chats, and summer visits; they include Jon Goldman and Megan Hester, Seema Shah and Sadruddin Chandani, Pierre Stroud and Marc Vogl, Gabriel Roth and Brian Perkins, Sandra Martinez, and Fauzia Khanani.

My family kept me sane, balanced, grounded, and focused during this whole enterprise. They give my life its true meaning and remind me about what's really important. My mother and father, Peggy and Ed O'Brien, taught me from an early age to be fiercely open to understanding the lives of other people, and I thank them for this invaluable and ongoing lesson. My stepfather Michael Tolaydo has been an energetic and supportive cheerleader throughout this whole process. My sister Beth always gives me a reason to smile and laugh, and I always feel better after I talk to her. My in-laws Farah Brelvi, David Ball, Shehnaz and Waseem Brelvi, and Marlon Banta, whom I love dearly, and my nieces and nephews Zaid, Aziz, and Soraya are a seemingly endless source of love, support, and hope for me.

My wife Saba Brelvi and my children Hamza, Shazia, and Nailah are my heart, my life, and my anchor. I am a fool for all of them, and they know it. They mean the world to me. Marrying Saba was the best decision I ever made, and my life is deeper, richer, and more meaningful than I ever imagined it could be because of her.

Finally, and most importantly, I thank God for making all of this possible, and for bestowing so many blessings upon me. Alhamdulillah.

Preface: Finding Everyday Muslim American Lives

1. Pew Research Center 2015: 2. According to this December 2015 survey, 46 percent of Americans believe the Islamic religion is more likely than other religions to encourage violence among its believers.

2. Kurzman 2016: 3. According to this 2016 report from the Triangle Center on Terrorism and Homeland Security, in 2015, thirty-nine Muslim Americans were linked to five plots to attack U.S. civilians. These plots resulted in nineteen fatalities, the bulk of which came from the fourteen victims of the San Bernardino, California, social service agency shooting that occurred in December 2015. Researchers have not agreed on a number for the U.S. Muslim population. My estimate of 3 million is based on averaging two different estimates—one of 2.6 million from the 2010 U.S. Religion Census sponsored by the Association of Statisticians of American Religious Bodies, and a second of 3.3 million from a 2016 estimate by the Pew Research Center; see Association of Statisticians of American Religious Bodies 2010; Pew Research Center 2016.

3. Brekhus 1998.

4. All names of people and places, and sometimes identifying characteristics such as ethnicity, have been changed to protect anonymity.

5. Tavory and Timmermans 2013.

6. Corsaro and Eder 1990.

7. Curtis 2009.

8. Jackson 2005; Marable and Aidi 2009; McCloud 2014.

9. Prickett 2014; Rouse 2004.

10. Asad 2009; Zubaida 2011.

Chapter One: The Culturally Contested Lives of Muslim Youth and American Teenagers

1. All names of people and places—including the group name "the Legendz"—as well as the particular ethnicities of some subjects, have been changed to protect anonymity.

2. Curtis 2009: 72–94.

3. Best 2006: 138; Garcia 2012: 99; Milner 2004: 53; Olsen 1997: 48–49, 147–48; Zhou and Bankston 1998: 161–71.

4. While others have used the terms "cultural system" or "cultural toolkit" to describe similar aggregations of cultural elements, I find that the term "cultural rubric" works best in portraying cultural reality as these Muslim teenagers—and others living lives characterized by multiple and somewhat demanding sets of expectations—experience it. Such a reality involves loosely aggregated sets of rules, behaviors, and

practices, each of which is associated with a socially meaningful group of others and vies for attention and allegiance from the individuals proximate to them. My conceptualization of "cultural rubrics" draws on the work of Carter 2005; Cornell 1996; Deeb and Harb 2013; Moerman 1965; Schielke 2009; Swidler 2001; and Zerubavel 1991.

5. On working mothers, see Blair-Loy 2003; Gerson 1986; Moen 1992. On second-generation immigrants, see, among others, Ajrouch 2004; Child 1943; Dhingra 2007; Gibson 1988; Kibria 1995; Smith 2005; and Zhou and Bankston 1998. On economically successful working-class people, see Sennett and Cobb 1972. On middle-class African American people, see Pattillo 1999 and Lacy 2007. On gay suburbanites, see Brekhus 2003. On religious scientists, see Ecklund 2010.

6. Best 2011; Bettie 2003; Coleman 1961; Eckert 1989; Milner 2004.

7. Milner 2004: 21. See also Eckert 1989.

8. Eckert 1989: 71 (emphasis mine).

9. Milner 2004: 37–38; Bettie 2003: 12; Coleman 1961: 173–90.

10. Anderson 2000: 35–37. See also Flores-Gonzáles 2002; Jones 2010.

11. Anderson 2000: 35.

12. Bettie 2003: 140; Anderson 2000: 65; Carter 2005: 52.

13. Carter 2005: 52; Pattillo 1999: 117–45.

14. Pattillo 1999: 93. See also Anderson 2000: 95–96; Carter 2005: 13, 61–64.

15. Espiritu 2003; Gibson 1988; Olsen 1997; Zhou and Bankston 1998.

16. Kibria 1995; Olsen 1997; Smith 2005.

17. Espiritu 2003: 169; Olsen 1997: 39, 147; Warikoo 2011: 49; Zhou and Bankston 1998: 215.

18. Pyke and Dang 2003.

19. Levitt 2009: 1,234; Olsen 1997: 55.

20. Kibria 1995: 9; LaBennett 2011: 120; Levitt 2009: 1,227; Olsen 1997: 148.

21. Fader 2009: 145–78; Peshkin 1986: 156–60; Rose 1988: 158–64; Wilkins 2008: 88–150.

22. Peshkin 1986: 158; Smith and Denton 2009: 141–43; Wilkins 2008: 97.

23. On the potential of being judged insufficiently religious by community adults and peers, see Fader 2009; Peshkin 1986; Rose 1988. On the significance of religious communal belonging to young people, see Ajrouch 2004; Lytch 2004; Peshkin 1986.

24. On young people moving more deeply into religiosity, see Davidman 1991; Pearce and Denton 2011: 127–31; Peek 2005; and Wilkins 2008: 88–150. On young people moving away from religion and into adolescent "deviance," see Fader 2009: 83–84; Lytch 2004: 126–34; Pearce and Denton 2011: 112–14; Peshkin 1986: 218–56; Smith and Denton 2009: 97–103.

25. Peshkin 1986: 143–49, 253–56; Lytch 2004: 99–119; Pearce and Denton 2011: 41–51; Smith and Denton 2009: 161–62.

26. Eckert 1989: 50.

27. Best 2011; Carter 2005; Pattillo 1999; Warikoo 2011.

28. Hebdige 2010; Milner 2004; Wilkins 2008.

29. Anderson 2000; Carter 2005; Eckert 1989; Pattillo 1999; Warikoo 2011; Wilkins 2008.

30. Anderson 2000: 95; Carter 2005: 35–36; Pattillo 1999: 135; Valenzuela 1999: 76–84; Warikoo 2011: 39–40, 118.

31. On behaviors, see Anderson 2000: 73; Bettie 2003: 14–15; Pattillo 1999: 130–35. On stories of ghetto adventure, see Pattillo 1999: 135–38.

32. Jeffries 2011: 116, 144.

33. Milner 2004: 53.

34. Warikoo 2004: 372; Smith 2005: 1,149–61.

35. Garcia 2012: 99.

36. Kibria 1995: 133–37.

37. Garcia 2012: 99; Peshkin 1986: 158; Smith and Denton 2009: 141–43; Wilkins 2008: 97.

38. Davidman 1991: 23; Fader 2009: 173–74; Peshkin 1986: 143–48; Wilkins 2008: 105–6.

39. Flory and Miller 2000: 141, 144; Peshkin 1986: 219; Wilkins 2008: 101.

40. Fader 2009: 130–34; Garcia 2012: 99; Peshkin 1986: 158; Smith and Denton 2009: 141–43; Wilkins 2008: 97.

Chapter Two: "Cool Piety"

1. Zhou and Bankston 1998.

2. Carter 2005: vi; Warikoo 2011: 117.

3. Perlmann and Waldinger 1997; Portes, Fernandez-Kelly, and Haller 2005; Kasinitz et al. 2008; Stepick and Stepick 2010.

4. Carter 2005: 109, 118; Kasinitz, Mollenkopf, and Waters 2004: 396.

5. Waters 1994: 807; Smith 2014: 531–39; Zhou and Bankston 1998: 198; Carter 2005: 55, 120.

6. Here I use a specific definition of assimilation used by Herbert Gans (1997), who defines the term to mean social integration, which differs from "acculturation," a term that implies cultural adaptation.

7. DeNora 2000.

8. Khabeer 2016; Aidi 2014.

9. Carter 2005: 13.

10. Peshkin 1986: 208; Warikoo 2011: 38–40; Valenzuela 1999: 83; Carter 2005: 61–64; Fader 2009: 164–66; Olsen 1997: 46; Lytch 2004: 103

11. Mohaiemen 2008.

12. Gosa 2011; Miyakawa 2005.

13. Cf. Aidi 2014.

14. See Frith 1996; Schütz 1951; Willis 2014.

15. Flores 2000; Harrison 2009: 101; LaBennett 2011: 121; Maira 2002; Rivera 2003; Sorett 2009; Vermurlen 2016; Warikoo 2011: 60.

16. Smith and Denton 2009: 141–43.

17. Fader 2009: 130–34; Garcia 2012: 99; Peshkin 1986: 158; Smith and Denton 2009: 141–43; Wilkins 2008: 97.

18. Best 2011: 914; Eckert 1989: 69; Milner 2004: 53.

19. Anderson 2000: 104; Pattillo 1999: 117–45; Ispa-Landa 2013: 8; Warikoo 2011: 35–40; Zhou and Bankston 1998: 185–215; Wilkins 2008: 28, 105–6.

20. Gans 1997.

21. Gans 1997.

22. Carter 2005: 109, 118; Kasinitz, Mollenkopf, and Waters 2004: 396.

23. Chang 2005: 445; Harrison 2009: 99–100; Kitwana 2002: 10; Warikoo 2011: 110–13.

24. George 1998; Rose 1994.

Chapter Three: "The American Prayer"

1. Deeb 2006; Deeb and Harb 2013; Mahmood 2005; Rouse 2004; Schielke 2009.
2. Bellah 1985; Espiritu 2003; Imoagene 2012; Zhou and Bankston 1998.
3. Comer 1993: 205; Milner 2004: 53; Patterson 2001; Zhou and Bankston 1998: 161–71.
4. Bellah 1985; Fischer 2008; Mahmood 2005; O'Brien 2015; Taylor 1985.
5. Beck, Giddens, and Lash 1994; Besecke 2001; Denzin 1975; Eickelman 1992; Fine 1979, 1987; Giddens 1991; Paden 1992; Roof 2001; Wilcox 2002.
6. For other, similar, cases of immigrant parents (and sometimes youth) interpreting young people's individualistic actions as evidence of them becoming more "American," see Gibson 1988: 195–98; Zhou and Bankston 1998: 161–71; Espiritu 2003: 157–78.
7. Goffman 1961: 85.
8. Goffman 1961: 108–9.
9. Willis 1977: 26–29; Warikoo 2011: 93; Eckert 1989: 60–61; Best 2006: 142–59.
10. Gibson 1988: 135; Peshkin 1986: 144; Fader 2009: 173.
11. Pascoe 2005.
12. Butler 1993: 3.
13. Butler 1993: 3.
14. Denzin 1975; Eickelman 1992; Fine 1979, 1987; Giddens 1991; Paden 1992.
15. Fader 2009: 130–34.
16. Peshkin 1986: 158.
17. Maghbouleh 2013.
18. Emirbayer and Mische 1998.
19. Mahmood 2005: 7.
20. Eliasoph and Lichterman 2003; Swidler 2001; Milner 2004: 53.
21. Peshkin 1986: 219.
22. Garcia 2012: 99.
23. Wilkins 2008: 101.
24. Bellah 1985.

Chapter Four: "Keeping It Halal" and Dating While Muslim

1. A similar tension has been observed among the diverse second-generation immigrant young women studied by Olsen 1997: 121–49; the Vietnamese American youth studied by Kibria 1995: 146–53; the Filipino American youth studied by Espiritu 2003: 157–78; and the young evangelical Christians studied by Irby 2014; Wilkins 2008; and Regnerus 2007.
2. Lainer-Vos 2013.
3. Garcia 2012: 98; Irby 2014: 270; Wilkins 2008: 133.
4. Regnerus 2007: 118
5. According to Regnerus, "abstinence pledgers . . . are idealists. They expect a lot from marriage and married sex, perhaps too much" (2007: 118). Irby's young evangelical Christian respondents also demonstrated a strong commitment to the notion of a religiously appropriate relationship, even in the face of visible failures by peers and others; Irby 2014: 270.
6. Brückner and Bearman 2005; Regnerus 2007; Irby 2014.
7. Regnerus respondent Leah spoke disparagingly of a Catholic "idealist" she knew, describing her as "just so naïve and like, she's like, 'everything's so perfect,' and, like,

can't do anything bad—wants to date somebody who's perfect. She won't kiss. She doesn't want to kiss anyone before she gets married because it has to be perfect, like [laughs] ... like marriage is ... the only perfect, holy thing you can share ... with each other. And it's mostly a religious thing"; Regnerus 2007: 97–98. Similarly, many of the young Latinas Garcia spent time with were critical of those who presented their virginity as a sign of their perfect religiosity or morality; Garcia 2012: 99.

8. Kimmel 2009: 197.

Chapter Five: On Being a Muslim in Public

1. Cainkar 2009; O'Brien 2011; Kohut 2011: 43–53.
2. Bettie 2003: 148–52; Carter 2005: 60–64; Jones 2010: 46–73.
3. Gibson 1988: 132–37; Olsen 1997: 37–57.
4. Best 2006; Wilkins 2008; Eckert 1989.
5. Wilkins 2008: 105–6; Flores-Gonzáles 2005: 638; Waters 1994: 807; Smith 2014: 531–39; Carter 2005: 55, 120.
6. Anderson 2000; Jones 2010; Warikoo 2011: 112–17.
7. Anderson 2000; Jones 2010; Flores-Gonzáles 2002: 71; Warikoo 2011: 112–16.

Chapter Six: Growing Up Muslim and American

1. Anderson 2000: 104; Pattillo 1999: 117–45; Ispa-Landa 2013: 8; Eckert 1989: 69; Milner 2004: 53; Warikoo 2011: 35–40; Zhou and Bankston 1998: 185–215.
2. Eckert 1989: 50.
3. Best 2000; Eckert 1989; Bettie 2003; Garcia 2012: 99; Wilkins 2008: 105–6.
4. Fader 2009: 130–34; Garcia 2012: 99; Maghbouleh 2013; Peshkin 1986: 158; Smith and Denton 2009: 141–43; Wilkins 2008: 97.
5. Brückner and Bearman 2005; Irby 2014; Regnerus 2007; Wilkins 2008: 116–49.
6. Bettie 2003: 148–52; Carter 2005: 60–64; Jones 2010: 46–73; Gibson 1988: 132–37.
7. Anderson 2000; Carter 2005: 55, 120; Coleman 1961: 43–50, 130–37; Flores-Gonzáles 2005: 638; Jones 2010; Smith 2014: 531–39; Warikoo 2011: 112–17; Waters 1994: 807; Wilkins 2008: 105–6.
8. Zubaida 2011.
9. Muhammad and Yusef were twenty-three, Abdul was twenty-one, and Tariq and Fuad were twenty.
10. Clydesdale 2007: 10–15.
11. Brown 2009: 4.
12. Arnett 2014.
13. Swidler 2001.
14. Bourdieu 1990.
15. For a review and critique of this argument, see Uecker, Regnerus, and Vaaler 2007.
16. For a similar situation of adult definitional power, see Zhou and Bankston 1998: 214–15.
17. Fine 1979, 1987; Corsaro and Eder 1990; Carter 2005; Tatum 2003.
18. Park and Miller 1969 [1921]: 237; Kasinitz, Mollenkopf, and Waters 2004: 189; Warner and Wittner 1998.

REFERENCES

Aidi, Hisham. 2014. *Rebel Music: Race, Empire, and the New Muslim Youth Culture.* New York: Pantheon.

Ajrouch, Kristine J. 2004. "Gender, Race, and Symbolic Boundaries: Contested Spaces of Identity Among Arab American Adolescents." *Sociological Perspectives* 47 (4): 371–91.

Anderson, Elijah. 2000. *Code of the Street: Decency, Violence, and the Moral Life of the Inner City.* New York: W. W. Norton.

Arnett, Jeffrey J. 2014. *Emerging Adulthood: The Winding Road from the Late Teens Through the Twenties.* New York: Oxford.

Asad, Talal. 2009. "The Idea of an Anthropology of Islam." *Qui Parle* 17 (2): 1–30.

Association of Statisticians of American Religious Bodies. 2010. "American Religious Data: 1952–2010." US Religion Census. Accessed October 23, 2016, at http://www.rcms2010.org/compare.php.

Beck, Ulrich, Anthony Giddens, and Scott Lash. 1994. *Reflexive Modernization: Politics, Tradition and Aesthetics in the Modern Social Order.* Stanford, CA: Stanford University Press.

Bellah, Robert N. 1985. *Habits of the Heart: Individualism and Commitment in American Life.* Berkeley: University of California Press.

Besecke, Kelly. 2001. "Speaking of Meaning in Modernity: Reflexive Spirituality as a Cultural Resource." *Sociology of Religion* 62 (3): 365–81.

Best, Amy L. 2000. *Prom Night: Youth, Schools, and Popular Culture.* New York: Routledge.

———. 2006. *Fast Cars, Cool Rides: The Accelerating World of Youth and their Cars.* New York: New York University Press.

———. 2011. "Youth Identity Formation: Contemporary Identity Work." *Sociology Compass* 5 (10): 908–22.

Bettie, Julie. 2003. *Women Without Class: Girls, Race, and Identity.* Berkeley: University of California Press.

Blair-Loy, Mary. 2003. *Competing Devotions: Career and Family Among Women Executives.* Cambridge, MA: Harvard University Press.

Bourdieu, Pierre. 1990. *The Logic of Practice.* Stanford, CA: Stanford University Press.

Brekhus, Wayne. 1998. "A Sociology of the Unmarked: Redirecting Our Focus." *Sociological Theory* 16 (1): 34–51.

———. 2003. *Peacocks, Chameleons, Centaurs: Gay Suburbia and the Grammar of Social Identity.* Chicago: University of Chicago Press.

Brown, Daniel W. 2009. *A New Introduction to Islam*. Chichester, UK: Wiley-Blackwell.

Brückner, Hannah, and Peter Bearman. 2005. "After the Promise: The STD Conse- quences of Adolescent Virginity Pledges." *Journal of Adolescent Health* 36 (4): 271–78.

Butler, Judith. 1993. *Bodies That Matter: On the Discursive Limits of "Sex."* New York: Routledge.

Cainkar, Louis A. 2009. *Homeland Insecurity: The Arab American and Muslim Ameri- can Experience After 9/11*. New York: Russell Sage Foundation.

Carter, Prudence L. 2005. *Keepin' It Real: School Success Beyond Black and White*. New York: Oxford University Press.

Chang, Jeff. 2005. *Can't Stop, Won't Stop: A History of the Hip-Hop Generation*. New York: St. Martin's Press.

Child, Irvin L. 1943. *Italian or American?: The Second Generation in Conflict*. New Haven, CT: Oxford University Press.

Clydesdale, Timothy T. 2007. *The First Year Out: Understanding American Teens After High School*. Chicago: University of Chicago Press.

Coleman, James S. 1961. *The Adolescent Society*. New York: Free Press.

Comer, James P. 1993. "The Potential Effects of Community Organization on the Future of Our Youth." In *Adolescence in the 1990s: Risk and Opportunity*, edited by R. Takanashi. New York: Teachers College Press.

Cornell, Stephen. 1996. "The Variable Ties That Bind: Content and Circumstance in Ethnic Processes." *Ethnic and Racial Studies* 19 (2): 265–89.

Corsaro, William A., and Donna Eder. 1990. "Children's Peer Cultures." *Annual Re- view of Sociology* 16:197–220.

Curtis, Edward E., IV. 2009. *Muslims in America: A Short History*. Oxford and New York: Oxford University Press.

Davidman, Lynn. 1991. *Tradition in a Rootless World: Women Turn to Orthodox Juda- ism*. Berkeley: University of California Press.

Deeb, Lara. 2006. *An Enchanted Modern: Gender and Public Piety in Shi'i Lebanon*. Princeton, NJ: Princeton University Press.

Deeb, Lara, and Mona Harb. 2013. "Choosing Both Faith and Fun: Youth Negotiations of Moral Norms in South Beirut." *Ethnos* 78 (1): 1–22.

DeNora, Tia. 2000. *Music in Everyday Life*. Cambridge: Cambridge University Press.

Denzin, Norman K. 1975. "Play, Games and Interaction: The Contexts of Childhood Socialization." *Sociological Quarterly* 16 (4): 458–78.

Dhingra, Pawan. 2007. *Managing Multicultural Lives: Asian American Professionals and the Challenge of Multiple Identities*. Stanford, CA: Stanford University Press.

Eckert, Penelope. 1989. *Jocks and Burnouts: Social Categories and Identity in the High School*. New York: Teachers College Press.

Ecklund, Elaine H. 2010. *Science vs. Religion: What Scientists Really Think*. New York: Oxford University Press.

Eickelman, Dale F. 1992. "Mass Higher Education and the Religious Imagination in Contemporary Arab Societies." *American Ethnologist* 19 (4): 643–55.

Eliasoph, Nina, and Paul Lichterman. 2003. "Culture in Interaction." *American Jour- nal of Sociology* 108 (4): 735–94.

Emirbayer, Mustafa, and Ann Mische. 1998. "What Is Agency?" *American Journal of Sociology* 103 (4): 962–1023.

Espiritu, Yen Le. 2003. *Home Bound: Filipino American Lives Across Cultures, Communities, and Countries.* Berkeley: University of California Press.

Fader, Ayala. 2009. *Mitzvah Girls: Bringing Up the Next Generation of Hasidic Jews in Brooklyn.* Princeton, NJ: Princeton University Press.

Fine, Gary A. 1979. "Small Groups and Culture Creation: The Idioculture of Little League Baseball Teams." *American Sociological Review* 44:733–745.

———. 1987. *With the Boys: Little League Baseball and Preadolescent Culture.* Chicago: University of Chicago Press.

Fischer, Claude S. 2008. "Paradoxes of American Individualism." *Sociological Forum* 23 (2): 363–72.

Flores, Juan. 2000. *From Bomba to Hip-Hop: Puerto Rican Culture and Latino Identity.* New York: Columbia University Press.

Flores-González, Nilda. 2002. *School Kids/Street Kids: Identity Development in Latino Students.* New York: Teachers College Press.

———. 2005. "Popularity Versus Respect: School Structure, Peer Groups and Latino Academic Achievement." *International Journal of Qualitative Studies in Education* 18 (5): 625–42.

Flory, Richard W., and Donald E. Miller. 2000. *GenX Religion.* New York: Routledge.

Frith, Simon. 1996. "Music and Identity." In *Questions of Cultural Identity*, edited by S. Hall and P. Du Gay. Thousand Oaks, CA: Sage.

Gans, Herbert J. 1997. "Toward a Reconciliation of 'Assimilation' and 'Pluralism': The Interplay of Acculturation and Ethnic Retention." *International Migration Review* 31 (4): 875–92.

Garcia, Lorena. 2012. *Respect Yourself, Protect Yourself: Latina Girls and Sexual Identity.* New York: New York University Press.

George, Nelson. 1998. *Hip Hop America.* New York: Penguin Books.

Gerson, Kathleen. 1986. *Hard Choices: How Women Decide About Work, Career and Motherhood.* Berkeley: University of California Press.

Gibson, Margaret A. 1988. *Accommodation Without Assimilation: Sikh Immigrants in an American High School.* Ithaca, NY: Cornell University Press.

Giddens, Anthony. 1991. *Modernity and Self-Identity: Self and Society in the Late Modern Age.* Stanford, CA: Stanford University Press.

Goffman, Erving. 1961. *Encounters: Two Studies in the Sociology of Interaction.* Indianapolis, IN: Bobbs-Merrill.

Gosa, Travis L. 2011. "Counterknowledge, Racial Paranoia, and the Cultic Milieu: Decoding Hip Hop Conspiracy Theory." *Poetics* 39 (3): 187–204.

Harrison, Anthony K. 2009. *Hip Hop Underground: The Integrity and Ethics of Racial Identification.* Philadelphia: Temple University Press.

Hebdige, Dick. 2010. *Subculture: The Meaning of Style.* London and New York: Routledge.

Imoagene, Onoso. 2012. "Being British vs. Being American: Identification Among Second-Generation Adults of Nigerian Descent in the US and UK." *Ethnic and Racial Studies* 35 (12): 2153–73.

Irby, Courtney A. 2014. "Dating in Light of Christ: Young Evangelicals Negotiating Gender in the Context of Religious and Secular American Culture." *Sociology of Religion* 75 (2): 260–83.

Ispa-Landa, Simone. 2013. "Gender, Race, and Justifications for Group Exclusion: Urban Black Students Bussed to Affluent Suburban Schools." *Sociology of Education* 86 (3): 218–33.

Jackson, Sherman A. 2005. *Islam and the Blackamerican: Looking Toward the Third Resurrection*. New York and Oxford: Oxford University Press.

Jeffries, Michael P. 2011. *Thug Life: Race, Gender, and the Meaning of Hip-Hop*. Chicago: University of Chicago Press.

Jones, Nikki. 2010. *Between Good and Ghetto: African American Girls and Inner-City Violence*. New Brunswick, NJ: Rutgers University Press.

Kasinitz, Philip, John H. Mollenkopf, and Mary C. Waters. 2004. *Becoming New Yorkers: Ethnographies of the New Second Generation*. New York: Russell Sage Foundation.

Kasinitz, Philip, John H. Mollenkopf, and Mary C. Waters. 2008. *Inheriting the City: The Children of Immigrants Come of Age*. New York: Russell Sage Foundation.

Khabeer, Su'ad Abdul. 2016. *Muslim Cool: Race, Religion, and Hip Hop in the United States*. New York: New York University Press.

Kibria, Nazli. 1995. *Family Tightrope: The Changing Lives of Vietnamese Americans*. Princeton, NJ: Princeton University Press.

Kimmel, Michael S. 2009. *Guyland: The Perilous World Where Boys Become Men*. New York: Harper.

Kitwana, Bakari. 2002. *The Hip Hop Generation: Young Blacks and the Crisis in African American Culture*. New York: Basic Civitas Books.

Kohut, Andy. 2011. *Muslim Americans: No Sign of Growth in Alienation or Support for Extremism*. Washington, DC: Pew Research Center.

Kurzman, Charles. 2016. *Muslim American Involvement with Violent Extremism, 2015*. Chapel Hill, NC: Triangle Center on Terrorism and Homeland Security.

LaBennett, Oneka. 2011. *She's Mad Real: Popular Culture and West Indian Girls in Brooklyn*. New York: New York University Press.

Lacy, Karyn R. 2007. *Blue-Chip Black: Race, Class, and Status in the New Black Middle Class*. Berkeley: University of California Press.

Lainer-Vos, Dan. 2013. "The Practical Organization of Moral Transactions: Gift Giving, Market Exchange, Credit, and the Making of Diaspora Bonds." *Sociological Theory* 31 (2): 145–67.

Levitt, Peggy. 2009. "Roots and Routes: Understanding the Lives of the Second Generation Transnationally." *Journal of Ethnic and Migration Studies* 35 (7): 1225–42.

Lytch, Carol E. 2004. *Choosing Church: What Makes a Difference for Teens*. Louisville, KY: Westminster John Knox Press.

Maghbouleh, Neda. 2013. "The Ta'Arof Tournament: Cultural Performances of Ethno-National Identity at a Diasporic Summer Camp." *Ethnic and Racial Studies* 36 (5): 818–37.

Mahmood, Saba. 2005. *Politics of Piety: The Islamic Revival and the Feminist Subject*. Princeton, NJ: Princeton University Press.

Maira, Sunaina. 2002. *Desis in the House: Indian American Youth Culture in New York City*. Philadelphia: Temple University Press.

Marable, Manning, and Hisham D. Aidi. 2009. *Black Routes to Islam*. New York: Palgrave Macmillan.

McCloud, Aminah, ed. 2014. *The Oxford Handbook of African American Islam*. Accessed September 12, 2016. doi: 10.1093/oxfordhb/9780199929269.001.0001.

Milner, Murray. 2004. *Freaks, Geeks, and Cool Kids: American Teenagers, Schools, and the Culture of Consumption*. New York: Routledge.

Miyakawa, Felicia M. 2005. *Five Percenter Rap: God Hop's Music, Message, and Black Muslim Mission*. Indianapolis: Indiana University Press.

Moen, Phyllis. 1992. *Women's Two Roles: A Contemporary Dilemma*. New York: Auburn House.

Moerman, Michael. 1965. "Ethnic Identification in a Complex Civilization: Who Are the Lue?" *American Anthropologist* 67 (5): 1215–30.

Mohaiemen, Naeem. 2008. "Fear of a Muslim Planet: Hip-Hop's Hidden History." In *Sound Unbound: Sampling Digital Music and Culture*, edited by P. D. Miller. London: MIT Press.

O'Brien, John. 2011. "Spoiled Group Identities and Backstage Work: A Theory of Stigma Management Rehearsals." *Social Psychology Quarterly* 74 (3): 291–309.

———. 2015. "Individualism as a Discursive Strategy of Action Autonomy, Agency, and Reflexivity Among Religious Americans." *Sociological Theory* 33 (2): 173–99.

Olsen, Laurie. 1997. *Made in America: Immigrant Students in our Public Schools*. New York: New Press.

Paden, William E. 1992. *Interpreting the Sacred: Ways of Viewing Religion*. Boston: Beacon Press.

Park, Robert Ezra, and Herbert Adolphus Miller. 1969 [1921]. *Old World Traits Transplanted*. New York: Arno Press.

Pascoe, Cheri J. 2005. "'Dude, You're a Fag': Adolescent Masculinity and the Fag Discourse." *Sexualities* 8 (3): 329–46.

Patterson, Orlando. 2001. "The American View of Freedom: What We Say, What We Mean." *Society* 38 (4): 37–45.

Pattillo, Mary E. 1999. *Black Picket Fences: Privilege and Peril Among the Black Middle Class*. Chicago: University of Chicago Press.

Pearce, Lisa, and Melinda L. Denton. 2011. *A Faith of Their Own: Stability and Change in the Religiosity of America's Adolescents*. New York: Oxford University Press.

Peek, Lori. 2005. "Becoming Muslim: The Development of a Religious Identity." *Sociology of Religion* 66 (3): 215–42.

Perlmann, Joel, and Roger Waldinger. 1997. "Second Generation Decline?: Children of Immigrants, Past and Present: A Reconsideration." *International Migration Review* 31 (4): 893–922.

Peshkin, Alan. 1986. *God's Choice: The Total World of a Fundamentalist Christian School*. Chicago: University of Chicago Press.

Pew Research Center. 2015. "Views of Government's Handling of Terrorism Fall to Post-9/11 Low." Washington, DC: Pew Research Center. Accessed November 1, 2016,

at http://www.people-press.org/2015/12/15/views-of-governments-handling-of
-terrorism-fall-to-post-911-low/.

———. "A New Estimate of the U.S. Muslim Population." Washington, DC: Pew Research Center. Accessed November 1, 2016, at http://www.pewresearch.org/fact
-tank/2016/01/06/a-new-estimate-of-the-u-s-muslim-population/.

Portes, Alejandro, Patricia Fernandez-Kelly, and William Haller. 2005. "Segmented Assimilation on the Ground: The New Second Generation in Early Adulthood." *Ethnic and Racial Studies* 28 (6): 1000–40.

Prickett, Pamela J. 2014. "Negotiating Gendered Religious Space: The Particularities of Patriarchy in an African American Mosque." *Gender & Society*: 29 (1): 51–72.

Pyke, Karen, and Tran Dang. 2003. "'FOB' and 'Whitewashed': Identity and Internalized Racism Among Second Generation Asian Americans." *Qualitative Sociology* 26 (2): 147–72.

Regnerus, Mark. 2007. *Forbidden Fruit: Sex and Religion in the Lives of American Teenagers.* Oxford: Oxford University Press.

Rivera, Raquel Z. 2003. *New York Ricans from the Hip Hop Zone.* New York: Palgrave Macmillan.

Roof, Wade C. 2001. *Spiritual Marketplace: Baby Boomers and the Remaking of American Religion.* Princeton, NJ: Princeton University Press.

Rose, Susan D. 1988. *Keeping Them Out of the Hands of Satan: Evangelical Schooling in America.* New York: Routledge.

Rose, Tricia. 1994. *Black Noise: Rap Music and Black Culture in Contemporary America.* Hanover, NH: University Press of New England.

Rouse, Carolyn. 2004. *Engaged Surrender: African American Women and Islam.* Berkeley: University of California Press.

Schielke, Samuli. 2009. "Being Good in Ramadan: Ambivalence, Fragmentation, and the Moral Self in the Lives of Young Egyptians." *Journal of the Royal Anthropological Institute* 15 (suppl. 1): S24–S40.

Schütz, Alfred. 1951. "Making Music Together: A Study in Social Relationship." *Sociological Research* 18:76–97.

Sennett, Richard, and Jonathan Cobb. 1972. *The Hidden Injuries of Class.* New York: Knopf.

Smith, Christian, and Melina L. Denton. 2009. *Soul Searching: The Religious and Spiritual Lives of American Teenagers.* New York: Oxford University Press.

Smith, Robert. 2005. *Mexican New York: Transnational Lives of New Immigrants.* Berkeley: University of California Press.

———. 2014. "Black Mexicans, Conjunctural Ethnicity, and Operating Identities in Long-Term Ethnographic Analysis." *American Sociological Review* 79 (3): 517–48.

Sorett, Josef. 2009. "'Believe Me, This Pimp Game Is Very Religious': Toward a Religious History of Hip Hop." *Culture and Religion* 10 (1): 11–22.

Stepick, Alex, and Carol D. Stepick. 2010. "The Complexities and Confusions of Segmented Assimilation." *Ethnic and Racial Studies* 33 (7): 1149–67.

Swidler, Ann. 2001. *Talk of Love: How Culture Matters.* Chicago: University of Chicago Press.

Tatum, Beverly. 2003. *Why Are All the Black Kids Sitting Together in the Cafeteria?* New York: Basic Books.

Tavory, Iddo, and Stefan Timmermans. 2013. "A Pragmatist Approach to Causality in Ethnography." *American Journal of Sociology* 119 (3): 682–714.

Taylor, Charles. 1985. *Philosophical Papers*, Vol. 2, *Philosophy and the Human Sciences.* Cambridge: Cambridge University Press.

Uecker, Jeremy E., Mark D. Regnerus, and Margaret L. Vaaler. 2007. "Losing My Religion: The Social Sources of Religious Decline in Early Adulthood." *Social Forces* 85 (4): 1667–92.

Valenzuela, Angela. 1999. *Subtractive Schooling: U.S.-Mexican Youth and the Politics of Caring.* Albany: State University of New York Press.

Vermurlen, Brad. 2016. "Structural Overlap and the Management of Cultural Marginality: The Case of Calvinist Hip-Hop." *American Journal of Cultural Sociology* 4 (1): 68–106.

Warikoo, Natasha K. 2004. "Cosmopolitan Ethnicity: Second-Generation Indo-Caribbean Identities." In *Becoming New Yorkers: Ethnographies of the New Second Generation*, edited by P. Kasinitz, J. H. Mollenkopf, and M. C. Waters. New York: Russell Sage Foundation.

———. 2011. *Balancing Acts: Youth Culture in the Global City.* Berkeley: University of California Press.

Warner, R. Stephen, and Judith Wittner. 1998. *Gathering in Diaspora: Religious Communities and the New Immigration.* Philadelphia: Temple University.

Waters, Mary C. 1994. "Ethnic and Racial Identities of Second-Generation Black Immigrants in New York City." *International Migration Review* 28 (4): 795–820.

Wilcox, Melissa M. 2002. "When Sheila's a Lesbian: Religious Individualism Among Lesbian, Gay, Bisexual, and Transgender Christians." *Sociology of Religion* 63 (4): 497–513.

Wilkins, Amy C. 2008. *Wannabes, Goths, and Christians: The Boundaries of Sex, Style, and Status.* Chicago: University of Chicago Press.

Willis, Paul E. 1977. *Learning to Labor: How Working Class Kids Get Working Class Jobs.* New York: Columbia University Press.

———. 2014. *Profane Culture.* Princeton, NJ: Princeton University Press.

Zerubavel, Eviatar. 1991. *The Fine Line: Boundaries and Distinctions in Everyday Life.* New York: Free Press.

Zhou, Min, and Carl Bankston. 1998. *Growing Up American: How Vietnamese Children Adapt to Life in the United States.* New York: Russell Sage Foundation.

Zubaida, Sami. 2011. *Beyond Islam: A New Understanding of the Middle East.* London and New York: I. B. Tauris.

INDEX

acculturation, 49, 166, 179n6
African American Muslims, xx
    rap and, 37–38, 41
agency, 53–55, 72–75
Aidi, Hisham D., 30
Al-Qaeda, ix–x
American youth culture, 10, 11–20, 53–54,
    68, 126, 150
    dating and, 80, 81–82, 86
    experimental phase, 157–59
    immigrant teens and, 13–14, 17–19, 27,
    119, 152
    religion and, 42, 59, 67, 75, 88
Anderson, Eli, 13, 15
assimilation, 27–30, 48, 179n6
autonomy, 47, 53–55, 58–62, 68, 70–72, 76,
    126, 148

Bellah, Robert, 77
Bourdieu, Pierre, 162
Brekhus, Wayne, x
Brown, Daniel, 160
Bukhari, Muhammad al-, 3, 4

Carter, Prudence, 37
category symbols, 16, 150
clarification practices, 88
"cool piety," 28, 29–30, 43–44, 49
culturally contested lives concept, xvii, 7,
    10–11, 17
    of Muslim American youth, 150, 164
cultural rubrics, xxii, 7, 9–11, 16–18, 153,
    177n4
cultural straddling, 37
"cultured capacities," 162

dating and courtship, 6, 19, 69, 78–111
    "dating while Muslim," 93–105
    "keeping it halal" dating, 84–93
discrimination. *See* harassment and
    discrimination

discursive individualism, 54, 76–77, 151

Eckert, Penelope, 12–13, 15, 16
"extreme Muslim" caricature, 54, 62–71,
    76, 151

female Muslim youth, xviii–xix, 65–66, 73
Five-Percent Nation, 38, 41

Gans, Herbert, 48–49, 179n6
Goffman, Erving, 58

hadith, xvi, 3, 9
halal behavior, 29, 81, 84, 86–96, 100, 106
    dating and, 84–93
    strategic ambiguity and, 98–101
    vs. *haram*, 29, 86, 98–101, 105, 157
harassment and discrimination, ix, 115, 116,
    117–18
    strategies against, 120–48
headscarves (*hijabs*), 2, 39–40, 62–63
hip hop, xvii, 6, 10, 17, 22–49
    "cool Muslim" listening to, 37–42
    "Islamic listening" to, 31–36, 41, 48
    "pivoting away from piety" and, 44–48

individualism (American), 53–55, 62
Islam
    American forms of, 8–9, 149–67
    "American prayer," 52–62
    five pillars of, 3–5
    "leading with," 129–35
    "low-key," 6, 82, 104–5, 115–19, 128, 135
    obligations of, 6, 9, 29, 53–77
    public identity and, 112–48
    "violence and," ix–x, 163
Islamic State (ISIS), ix–x, 163
Islamophobia. *See* harassment and
    discrimination

Khabeer, Su'ad Abdul, 30